Praise for *The Secret Language of the Heart*

"Powerful, wisdom-filled, and practical! *The Secret Language of the Heart* is *the* go-to manual for awakening the power of the heart in love, healing, and everyday life!"

—**Gregg Braden**,
New York Times best-selling author
of *The Divine Matrix* and *Deep Truth*

"*The Secret Language of the Heart* is a very special gift on how to use music, sound, and vibrational tools to optimize your mind and body. Barry Goldstein is not only a talented musician, he's also a great communicator who gives you step-by-step instructions on how to use sound to feel more focused, relaxed, creative, and happier overall. I highly recommend it."

—**Daniel G. Amen, MD**,
founder of Amen Clinics and *New York Times*
best-selling author of *Change Your Brain, Change Your Life*

"A wonderful book that cannot help but be a joy to all who have the good fortune to read it."

—**Neale Donald Walsch**,
New York Times best-selling author of *Conversations with God*

"In this powerful yet user-friendly guide, Barry Goldstein maps out and defines the important role of music, sound, and vibration in creating heart and brain coherence. *The Secret Language of the Heart* provides innovative tools, solid research, and compassionate insight to fuel the creation of your own daily music program and is a reminder that the intersection where science and spirituality meet lays at the crossroads of your heart."

—**Deborah Rozman, PhD**,
president and co-CEO of HeartMath

"*The Secret Language of the Heart* unveils the true blueprint of music beyond art and entertainment as a vehicle for coming home to the heart and optimal health. Barry and his work are both passionate and filled with love."

—**Don Miguel Ruiz**,
author of *New York Times* best seller *The Four Agreements*

"After twenty-seven years of experiencing great music through vibration, I know that music is the language of the soul and can assist the mind in reaching inner divinity. In *The Secret Language of the Heart*, Goldstein creates that great meaning of great music."
—C. Norman Shealy, MD, PhD,
founder and CEO of the National Institute of Holistic Medicine and editor of the *Journal of Comprehensive Integrative Medicine*

"In *The Secret Language of the Heart*, Barry Goldstein creates a roadmap with music as a vehicle for journeying back to and grounding into our authentic self. I love his music and would highly recommend his work to anyone seeking to go deeper into the realms of his or her own heart, mind, and soul!"
—Anita Moorjani,
New York Times best-selling author of *Dying To Be Me*

"The employment of pharmaceuticals, nutraceuticals, and electroceuticals are instrumental in healing the heart. The brilliant work of Barry Goldstein has now created "acousticeuticals," an entirely new field to open the heart. The many forms of music, sound, vibration, and acoustics that Barry Goldstein recommends support heart rate variability (HRV), which in essence reveals the truth of the heart-brain connection. *The Secret Language of the Heart* is a must read to learn how to access musical gateways for cardiac rejuvenation and renewal."
—Dr. Stephen Sinatra,
board-certified cardiologist and author

"Barry Goldstein's new book takes the healing power of music, sound, and vibration to a whole new level of transformation for your body, mind, and spirit!"
—John Holland,
spiritual medium

"Seldom does one find so much life-changing wisdom in such a small and readable volume. Now I know that as I explore the scientific basis of sound and music healing I can fine-tune my creativity and enjoyment with well-chosen music. And what a difference it makes! This book is a masterpiece and will make a big difference in the lives of many people. Thank you, Barry!"
—James L. Oschman, PhD,
author of *Energy Medicine*

"*The Secret Language of the Heart* provides a significant new approach to creating harmony and balance within by using the power of the heart's song. Barry Goldstein blends modern and ancient sound techniques with holistic counseling to completely transform stress and heal the body. This book empowers readers to experience the compassion so necessary for the evolution of our consciousness in today's world."

—**Dr. Darren R. Weissman,**
developer of the LifeLine Technique and best-selling author of
The Power of Infinite Love & Gratitude

"*The Secret Language of the Heart* awakens and activates the unsung song of the heart and brings us to coherence between mind, heart, and nature. Barry Goldstein has done an amazing job of capturing the tools to begin this magnificent journey of becoming the music that we are."

—**Dr. Sue Morter,**
founder of the Morter Institute for Bioenergetics

"In *The Secret Language of the Heart*, Barry Goldstein provides easy yet profound steps in creating a heart-centered program to improve your health and quality of life. Whether you are a musician or not, now you can lead a life filled with harmony!"

—**Colette Baron-Reid,**
author, intuitive, medium, musician, and artist

"For thousands of years, music has been a language that speaks to the heart. In *The Secret Language of the Heart*, Barry Goldstein gives us a sound program to fine-tune our heart awareness and listen to music in a new way—from the inside out. A modern program incorporating ancient wisdom!"

—**Don Miguel Ruiz Jr.,**
author of *The Five Levels of Attachment*

"This book is genius! A brilliant resource and dynamic hands-on guide to crafting your own harmony of living, with vibrant health and the wisdom from within our own hearts."

—**Heather McCloskey Beck,**
author of *Take the Leap*

"I love this book. Barry has composed a symphony of stories and scientific research explaining how the vibrations of music can heal your life and transform your heart."

—Andy Dooley,
creator of Vibration Activation

"This jewel of a book is extraordinary in its simplicity and depth. I stress simplicity because a true master has the ability to take something complex and make it seem simple. Barry Goldstein is truly a master musician, and by spending time with this book you will come to appreciate and embrace music in ways you've never imagined."

—Blaine Bartlett,
speaker, author, consultant, executive, and leadership coach

"Barry Goldstein is one of the most innovative musical minds to surface in the area of transformation and healing. Understanding the creative process, he has discovered new ways to release the blocks that we experience and create the flow that should be part of our nature. I am a huge fan and have employed many of his techniques to create a harmonious balance for both healing and creating joy."

—Robert Cutarella,
two-time Grammy Award–winning producer

"A timely and compelling read. I wondered what the next revealing, unique, and purposeful book would be that was in alignment and harmony with the new world in which we live. *The Secret Language of the Heart* is it."

—Maureen Moss,
author, consciousness teacher, and catalyst for change

"Barry's exploration of sound and vibration and their uses to create more vibrancy and healing in everyday life is exceptional!"

—Sarah McLean,
director of the McLean Meditation Institute

"The healing that occurs when you open up to the vibration of music is something I have experienced firsthand. I love that Barry Goldstein has bridged the gap between science and spirituality through the one language we all can understand . . . music! *The Secret Language of the Heart* provides musical prescriptions for a more healthy and joy-filled life and is a must read."

—Sunny Dawn Johnston,
author of *The Love Never Ends* and *Invoking the Archangels*

The Secret Language *of the* Heart

The
Secret
Language
of the
Heart

How to Use Music, Sound, and Vibration
as Tools for Healing and Personal Transformation

BARRY GOLDSTEIN

Hier**⊕**phantpublishing

Cover design by Emma Smith
Cover art by Stokkete | Shutterstock
Interior design by Steve Amarillo
Illustrations by John Dispenza

Hierophant Publishing
8301 Broadway, Suite 219
San Antonio, TX 78209
888-800-4240
www.hierophantpublishing.com

If you are unable to order this book from your local bookseller,
you may order directly from the publisher.

Library of Congress Control Number: 2016931682
ISBN: 978-1-938289-43-9
10 9 8 7 6 5 4 3 2 1
Printed on acid-free paper in the United States of America

To Donese, the song of my heart

Contents

Foreword

I GREW UP PLAYING THE PIANO. As part of my daily routine between homework and sports activities, it was a very firm requirement that I practice piano for at least one hour after school. I'd start each session by running my fingers up and down the keys, playing all of the scales—both sharps and flats. Then I would hammer out all of the chords that I knew in every key—major, minor, dominant, half diminished, and fully diminished. And if I made a mistake, I'd hear a stomp thundering from the ceiling, as if God was listening to me from above. Of course, I knew that I had to start all over again from the beginning and not rush through the sequences. Once my fingers were totally connected to my brain, I would do my best to master a classical piece composed by Chopin, Bach, Beethoven, or Brahms.

Upon reflection, I think those eight years of my childhood were more of a prison sentence than a sign of creative ambition. It was only in the last few years that I was allowed to play jazz, blues, pop, or rock and roll. As you can imagine, being a young kid, playing anything other than classical music was liberating. For hours I'd watch in awe as Elton John and Billy Joel played the ivories with such command, such passion, and such grace—and they never made a mistake or needed to look at the keys. As a result, I wanted only one thing: to play without ever looking at my hands, and, at the same time, to possess the ability to improvise into some creative, altered state of mind.

It never happened. My interests changed. I became more involved in academia, a social life, and high school sports. After all, there are only so many hours in a day. My father was disappointed I didn't continue studying piano, and he would always say the same thing when I fought him with the resistance of any male adolescent with elevated testosterone levels: "One day you will wish you never stopped." He was right.

When I met Barry Goldstein many years ago, I fell in love with him and his music. He is an award-winning musician with a unique talent and skill for making music, sound, vibration, and coherence all come together for us. He is a true composer, a modern-day classical artist with sensitivity for moving the hearts and souls of all who have the ears to hear. He has touched my mind, my heart, and my soul in so many ways with his various masterpieces. Meeting him and listening to his tunes has rekindled my enthusiasm for music. Plus, he's cool.

I have had the privilege of leading large workshops around the world teaching people how to use meditation to change their internal states, to heal themselves of various maladies, and to create better lives for themselves. The model of transformation that I use combines the principles of quantum physics, neuroscience, neuroendocrinology, psychoneuroimmunology, and epigenetics. I believe that science has become the contemporary language of mysticism.

Theses are big words, but don't be intimidated. Each of these fields points the finger at possibility and suggests that we are not doomed by our genes or hardwired to be a certain way for the rest of our lives. They propose that we have control of our destiny, that we are marvels of adaptability, and that we can change at any age. I have witnessed true miracles in people's lives when they apply and personalize these theories into practical experience.

This is where Barry Goldstein comes in. He is a major orchestrator of those conditions in our seminars. Barry and I have been working together for over three years. He has played live music during the meditations in our five-day advanced workshops. We have over five hundred people attending these events from all over the world and have completed a total of nine events to date. The type of meditations we do vary depending on what we are intending to accomplish. Some last one hour, some two hours, and some even three hours—and we do three meditations per day. Each one is always different, and so is the music our participants hear.

You have to imagine this. The lights are very low and hundreds of people are sitting, eyes closed, in a large ballroom. Barry is on stage with me, sitting at his keyboard. He is watching me (not looking down at his keys) and we are improvising. It's my childhood dream, but I'm not playing. Barry is, because he's a master of his craft.

I actually don't know how all of this unfolds, but I can tell you all I am doing is making hand signals while staring into Barry's eyes. And he is intuitively playing music and making the right sounds that quickly change our students' brain waves from a state of wakefulness into a state of transcendence; that alter the type of brain waves they produce to become more coherent and synchronized; that sustain those brain states for extended periods of time; that quiet the analytical mind and lower the volume to intrusive thoughts; that help open their hearts so they can embrace more elevated emotions, causing their hearts to beat in a more orderly and coherent manner, which then begins to produce a strong magnetic signal from that part of the body; that inspire them to transform some aspect of their limited beliefs; and, most importantly, that enable them to get beyond themselves.

I bet you are wondering how I know that all of these phenomena are occurring. It's simple. I have a team of researchers and scientists who measure our students' biological changes during our advanced events. We do regular quantitative studies on the brain (EEG), the heart (HRV and EKG), the energy of the room (GDV), and the energy emitted around people's bodies (GDV). So I know that Barry's music makes our students' brains work better, enhances the energy fields surrounding their bodies, and enriches the ambient energy field of the ballroom. And his recipes of sounds and tones have created more measureable heart coherence, as you will learn in this book.

Our research has shown that a clear intention (which is an act of a focused and coherent mind), coupled with an elevated emotion like joy, gratitude, care, wholeness, freedom, and compassion (which is a function of the heart) changes people's states of being. Barry's music is the necessary component for the process.

Barry has taken my audiences into elegant and deep states of mind. He has regularly composed music to transcend this reality. His original music helps our students get beyond their bodies, disconnect from their environment, and forget about time. That's when the magic happens. By artfully filling the space of the room with rhythmic vibrations, tones, sounds, and energetic waves, Barry helps everyone forget that their outer world exists. Only when the inner world is more real than the outer world can the brain and body change form. Barry's music seduces us into those transcendent, blissful realms.

So take your time. Maybe turn on some of his music. And read this book with an open mind and heart. Barry's certainly done his homework to educate you about the world of sound and vibration. He has also given you ways to let go of anything that stands in the way of you and your true potential. I hope you enjoy this book as much as I have.

—Dr. Joe Dispenza
New York Times best-selling author of *You Are the Placebo* and *Breaking the Habit of Being Yourself*

Note to Readers

This book is not intended as a substitute for medical advice of your physician. The reader should consult a physician in matters relating to his/her health and particularly with respect to any symptoms that may require diagnosis or medical attention.

Preface

MUSIC IS A LANGUAGE that has spoken to me my entire life. From the time I picked up the guitar and learned three chords, I've been passionate about writing songs. I remember sitting on the edge of my bed creating vocal melodies over chord progressions. It was official: I was in love! Music was always a vehicle for me to share my heart, and at the same time it touched mine. Although I did not know it at the time, it was within my musical process that my spiritual practice evolved. Music set the foundation for a harmonious love affair that provided the perfect balance of giving and receiving with something beyond myself.

As my aspirations to become a professional musician manifested, something changed. Somewhere along the way, as music became my livelihood, it also became a job. In 1997, I came to the realization that I needed to make a change. I'd been working as a musician and record producer in New York City for ten years, and the process of creating a four-minute song was taking an average of fifty to a hundred hours. Between composing, producing, and dealing with record company executives and recording artists, my love for music was getting lost in the process. Something was missing.

I longed to reconnect with my love for music and take it into a new realm, but I didn't know where to start. How could I reconnect with that twelve-year-old boy within, the one who sat on the edge of his bed writing songs in pure bliss? I was at a crossroads, at the intersection where it all started: my heart. This is where my love for music was birthed, and I knew this was where it needed to be rebirthed.

I began seeking answers on the Internet, and I remember typing *music* and *heart* into a search engine. I'm not sure exactly what I was looking for in that moment, but I learned that a human heart in a relaxed state beats about 60 times per minute. I knew that the measurement of beats per minute was used in music to designate how fast or slow a piece of music moved (tempo). This prompted me to incorporate the tempo of 60 beats per minute into some of my compositions with the intention that the pulse of the music would take me to a more relaxed, present state where I could reconnect with my heart, my passion, and my love for music. In addition, I was curious what would happen if I just allowed the music to move through me and speak to me as opposed to formally composing it. This process of listening and trusting my musical intuition at a new level excited me! This was the beginning of allowing music, the secret language of the heart, to speak to me once again. This time, it went beyond listening with "all ears"; it was with "all heart!"

This was a journey of moving back into harmonic alignment with my heart, and within it I discovered a new process of creating. Instead of composing, as I'd done for so many years, I was now de-composing music. From a state of relaxation, both mental and physical, I rediscovered my love for music. I began each new piece with the intention that it would serve the highest capacity of healing for each individual listening, starting with myself. And it did. I found myself moving to deep meditative states, and at the same time it was very rejuvenating. The stressed-out, type-A New Yorker who'd lost his passion for music began to disappear, and in this healing a new way of creating music evolved. I began to build layers within the music based solely on my intuition, never knowing what chords or melodies would come next. This painted some unique harmonics, combining layers of notes and frequencies that felt otherworldly. While I was used to being "in the zone" while composing in the past, this was different from anything I had ever created.

As I composed these pieces, it felt like my heartbeat and the music I was producing in the studio were perfectly in sync. This is the very definition of entrainment; an internal rhythm (my heartbeat) syncing with an external rhythm (the music). When this occurs, it can create an orderly heart rhythm (coherence) that has many health benefits. In addition, this new process took the pressures that occurred in my mind out of the picture and allowed me to become a vehicle for a unique synergy with a greater power to manifest a sacred co-creation. In this unique process of reaching a relaxed state through creating music, my body, mind, and spirit moved back into balance.

I believe this music achieved success so effortlessly because listeners felt the intention that was embedded within. It also assisted my healing process and overall health on many levels: my stress levels decreased significantly, my body was less tense, and I was sleeping more soundly. The pieces I created while in this state went on to become my CD series *Ambiology*, and the music, sound, and vibration of this series are assisting people with sleep disorders, anxiety, stress, brain harmony, focus, and clarity, as well as shifting the environment.

It was these successes that created a thirst for understanding why my music was working from a scientific basis. At the time, Dr. Donese Worden (who is now my fiancée) was using my music to treat insomnia in her patients. She encouraged and assisted me in researching the benefits of how music can be used to treat specific medical conditions. It became a unique relationship that was kind of like Reese's Peanut Butter Cups—I got my music in her medicine, and she got her medicine in my music. After researching for three years, I began to lecture at medical conferences on music's ability to benefit specific conditions, and we are now conducting research studies to determine the health benefits of my music.

In addition, implementing a musical program into my own life allowed me to reclaim my energy, clarify my purpose, and provide me with the focus to reach new levels of success, including coproducing a Grammy Award–winning track with Les Paul, the inventor of the solid body electric guitar.

The Native Americans have a saying: "The longest journey you will ever take is from your mind to your heart." As my spiritual path has developed over the past twenty years, I have uncovered more and more information that supports my experience of how music can be used as a vehicle for healing, to ignite creative energy and to guide us back to our hearts. Whether you are creating a piece of art, writing a business plan, or redecorating your home, you can make your creative process more sacred, put your mind more at ease, and improve your physical health through the conscious and consistent use of music.

Each of our lives can be a beautiful song. The same principles that create this song can be utilized to create a magnificent life. We can bring harmony into our relationships, find rhythm in our careers, and provide sound advice to friends and loved ones. We can orchestrate new opportunities, compose new ideas, and conduct our lives with integrity. At the same time, we can learn to remove dissonance from challenging situations, arrange our energy more effectively, and learn to listen beyond just hearing. We are meant to live a musical life.

Introduction

Musical training is a more potent instrument than any other, because rhythm and harmony find their way into the inward places of the soul, imparting grace, and making the soul of him who is rightly educated graceful.

—Plato

IT'S HARD TO SAY WHEN I FIRST realized music could be a transformational tool. I remember sitting on our piano bench, feet dangling with the floor miles away, as my mother sat next to me, her feet dangling too. My mom was only four feet five inches tall, but she had the spirit of a giant. I was two or three then, but I remember how each note filled the room as my mother sang the playful Harry Belafonte song "Yellow Bird." As she sang, her small fingers lay gently on top of mine, striking the keys in time with each note she sang. I sat in wide-eyed wonder as I felt the vibration of the piano notes matching her voice. This is what I now know to be resonance, her voice's vibration magnifying the vibration of the piano note. Even after the notes played, they hung in the air, like a beautiful hummingbird sharing its song. The notes changed the room, as did the space between the notes. Both were so beautiful, and when they stopped the room felt so empty.

I think it was then that I seeded a longing to fill the room with music and to feel the space between the notes. My mom was never formally trained in music; she played by ear, and she informally passed this gift on to me. She knew then that music is to be felt by the heart. I can still feel her tiny fingers on top of mine guiding me over the ivory keys, guiding me through my first transformational experience with music. My heart is filled with gratitude for her gift to me: sharing the power of song to shift ordinary moments into life-altering experiences.

It is in this vibration of gratitude that I would like to begin our journey together into the secret language of the heart. I am so thankful to have the opportunity to share a beautiful gift that all of us have been given access to. We have opened this gift at many times in our lives and have been blessed to have it touch our souls on a deep level. Music has always been there, from our first lullaby and first kiss to the prom dance, sweet sixteen, breakups and makeups, weddings, anniversaries, baby showers—virtually every important moment of our lives. While friends may come and go, careers may shift, and hair may disappear over the years, music will always be here. Thank you, music!

Music is a common chord that weaves through every culture, speaking to us in a secret language, a language from and of the soul, one that speaks beyond reason, race, and religion. Music defines the indefinable and gives meaning to the tapestry of moments woven together to create our lives. These moments define our soul's path and how our unique vibration ripples outward in the world.

That is why music is here: to communicate what words cannot, and to assist in integrating the wisdom of our minds and the lessons of our hearts for the purpose of our personal and spiritual evolution. When we can see music in this light, it becomes more than just art and entertainment; it is a translator of divine thought, and a way of life. It is a powerful vehicle to transform us on the deepest level, from the inside out.

In this book, we will tap into music's known power as art and entertainment and also move beyond that to unleash its full potential to enhance and improve our health and quality of life. If your soul has been longing for something to truly touch your heart and assist you, look no further. Music is here for you. As we bring awareness to music, sound, and vibration on a daily basis, we experience it in a new way—internally to externally. There is music that exists inside your physical body. It is a precious gift never to be taken for granted, for it is your own unique sound and vibration that communicates to you beyond words, as you will soon learn.

When we talk about utilizing music to improve our health, it is not just the physical body we are talking about. To get the full picture of health, we must look at the four-body system: the physical, mental, emotional, and spiritual bodies. Each has a unique role in our total health. Throughout the book, you will hear me refer to this concept as *the four bodies*.

Music has the potential to transform, but change is not always an easy thing, for change needs to initiate from a deeper level. Change must move past the surface, past our limited emotions, beliefs, and negative patterns. It must move beyond our physicality and our programming of the mind. For true transformation to occur, change must immerse itself in our being; it must touch our heart and soul. That's what we'll work on in the course of this book, with music as a conduit.

What to Expect from This Book

We'll start by discussing the music that is within each and every one of us—our heartbeat, our breath, and our sigh. From there, we'll learn how music and sound can affect the body and the brain. Armed with this knowledge, we'll implement a daily practice that has you using music strategically throughout your day to boost your mental, physical, emotional, and spiritual health. Music is a power tool that can improve, redesign, and reignite your day.

Another key thing I want you to take away from this book is the importance of having a daily music practice. To help you get started, each chapter has tips, exercises, and techniques you can incorporate into your practice to suit your needs. I encourage you to try each one at least once, and keep the ones that work best for you.

Sound Tools for Transformation

The end of each chapter provides additional tools that allow you to integrate the topics and information into your life through an experience. Reading is much different than applying your knowledge, and I encourage you to have your own unique experiences bringing each chapter into your life.

Suggested Music

One of the most challenging things about writing a book about music is that there is no actual music in it. To remedy this, I have suggested music in most of the chapters that complements the subject matter. I have handpicked this music after seeing what has assisted people on a daily basis for over fifteen years. In some cases, I have suggested my own compositions when they have had a proven beneficial track record on the specific topic at hand.

Don't just zip through the book. Utilize the suggested music as a tool to integrate the information provided in each chapter. This moves you beyond just thinking about the topic and allows you to experience it, feel it in your mind, body, and soul, and integrate it. This is one of music's wonderful gifts; it allows us to integrate wisdom and knowledge. There is also suggested music for the experiential processes that will elevate your experience.

Experience

Everything I have learned about music, sound, and vibration over the last forty years has been seeded by an experience. These experiences have transformed my life, ignited my curiosity, and inspired me to form my own hypotheses that I am excited to share with you here. I believe that inspiration creates inspiration, and I hope my stories and research will inspire new creative adventures for you as well.

Research

Even before the times of Pythagoras, music and the sciences have danced hand in hand. Along with my personal experience, I've also cited numerous studies to show that these assertions of music's innate power have scientific legs. There is still much more work to be done on the effects of music on our health, creativity, and peace of mind, but the research presented here will help deepen your understanding of this emerging field of study.

Of course, the suggestions you have just read are geared toward optimizing your experience. One of the major points of this book is to discover what resonates with you. The intention is that you utilize this book to become an expert on what feels sound to your instrument—your physical, mental, emotional, and spiritual bodies.

It's time to rejuvenate and replenish our souls. It's time to stop holding back our gifts on any level. It's time to share ourselves in the world, for we are so needed. It's time to tune up and tune in to create a new song of harmony, peace, love, compassion, and kindness.

Just as creating a meditative practice can change your life, so can creating a musical practice. This does not mean you have to be a musician, but it does mean you can incorporate music into your life with intention to create transformation. Incorporating the information, tools, exercises, and musical suggestions contained here will help you to manage your daily stresses, enhance your creativity, and master your emotional and physical well-being. Are you ready to create that shift? Then let's begin!

PART ONE

Music *as a* Healing Tool

The Music Within

Music in the soul can be heard by the universe.

—Lao Tzu

AS YOU SHALL SOON SEE, music, sound, and vibration are powerful tools to create expansion and healing. One of the reasons that music can be such a strong vehicle for transformation is its ability to shift our emotions in a positive way. When we can transform our emotions or remove an emotional block, we open the door for healing to occur. Many of us affect our health negatively on a daily basis by either ignoring or not bringing awareness to our emotions. Ongoing negative emotions can impact our physical, mental, emotional, and spiritual bodies—even if we are unaware of them.

Even if I start my day in a relaxed state from meditating, listening to music, or playing my guitar, it's not unusual for me to get to my recording studio twenty minutes later stressed. A lot can happen in a twenty-minute walk to work in New York City! Walking down six floors of stairs, horns honking on Eighth Avenue, stepping in dog poo, police sirens, homeless people asking for money, rain and no umbrella, only one elevator working in the recording studio, the computer not booting up . . . Talk about stimulating your five senses! And this is before my workday really starts.

Upon getting to the studio and checking my messages, I learn that a project that was due at the end of the week is now being moved up to tomorrow. With the inevitable prospect of an all-night recording session, I begin to feel some anxiety. I need to schedule singers to get the background vocals done and find a bass player at the last minute. It all begins to paint a not-so-pretty and stressful picture. As I dive into my work, I begin to feel tightness in my neck, and an uneasy feeling in my stomach. *My emotions are beginning to affect my physical body.*

In addition, I feel a bit nervous and notice my usual patience in situations has diminished. As my day unfolds, I find myself snapping at people. A situation that I normally would have let pass elevates into an angry argument. *My emotions are beginning to affect my mental body.*

The walk I take in Central Park during my lunch break is blown off and replaced by a phone call to a friend where I vent and relive my stressful morning. The deeper connection and faith that I usually feel while being in nature is now absent in my day. *My emotions are beginning to affect my spiritual body.*

After an all-night recording session, I send the final mix to the record company and release a big sigh. I notice how much stress I was holding as the sound of my breath is released, and I notice how much lighter I feel.

What if the stressful day that I had is a typical reoccurring day? The only things that change are the situations, but the stress is never managed. This ongoing unawareness of how our emotions effect our physical, mental, and spiritual bodies can lead to such challenges as lower back pain, insomnia, high blood pressure, disease, anxiety, and depression. Any one of these could make a person feel incomplete or out of balance, the feeling and state of being unhealthy.

Your challenging day may be different. Maybe you are under some financial stress; maybe you are going through a tough breakup; or perhaps a loved one has recently passed. Every one of these situations can have many different levels of stress that can snowball into challenges in our four bodies—spiritual, mental, emotional, and physical—and our overall health.

The good news is that the opposite is true as well. Positive emotional states can benefit our physical, mental, and spiritual well-being. The healing process is all about moving back into balance and returning to our natural state of wholeness. Not just finding a cure, but finding our health.

Music can provide an antidote to our venomous emotional states if we become aware of the healing power that it holds. Music is more than just a song on a radio; it is a language that exists inside you, and one that you can tap into to alleviate emotional stressors that challenge your spiritual, mental, emotional, and physical health. By using music, sound, and vibration, we can bring our four bodies back into balance, and create space for deep healing.

As you can see, I needed a tool to combat stress on a daily basis. I needed a way to come back home to my heart in a short period of time. The processes I will share in this chapter helped me to re-center and bring a knowing that as long as I have my heartbeat, my breath, and my sigh, everything is truly okay. In finding this knowing, I am able to shift to a state of gratitude where the smaller daily challenges melt away into the "sound" breathing processes. I have a path to move into the sacred process of creation with clear heart, clear mind, and clear intentions.

There is an amazing power that the sounds within us contain. We will begin to tap into their ability to act as a catalyst to release negative emotions, mental blocks, and physical stress on a regular basis. I have incorporated them into my own daily program to jump-start my four bodies in their innate ability to heal, and I have personally seen amazing results. Since I have implemented these breathing techniques into my life, I very rarely have a day like the one I shared with you earlier. I know that these breathing techniques will be a powerful transformational tool in your days and life as well! They are an invitation to you to come back home to your heart.

Internal Music

The music within, or our *internal music*, is always with us. It is the music that is created from our bodies themselves through three sources: the sacred heartbeat, the breath, and sigh. Each person's internal music is a unique symphony within that is calling out for us to listen and is communicating the needs of the four bodies. Internal music is also a helpful tool for dealing with daily stressors, as your internal music is always with you and available to you.

We can use the sacred heartbeat, breath, and sigh to create, cultivate, and induce our four bodies' healing patterns. Ultimately, we are the true conductors of these instruments that create our foundation for how we manage our health and quality of life.

The Sacred Heartbeat

Just as the drums and rhythm section create the musical foundation for how we synchronize and entrain to a musical piece, the heartbeat is our internal rhythm that synchronizes us to inner peace. It is this same sound that connects us to each other and to the rhythm of everything in the universe while we are in our bodies. The sound and vibration of our heartbeat is a symbol that we are alive in this moment.

By coming home to your heart, you tap into your heart's

magnificent vibration and its music. The more you listen to your heart, literally, the more it speaks back to you. It sends messages to you during your decision-making processes. Maybe you've noticed an uneasy feeling in your stomach or something telling you not to move forward in a situation. Maybe you got goose bumps or chills when a song affected you in a profound way. Your heart is constantly singing a secret language to you, calling out and sending signals for you to listen. And when you do, it is life changing!

The Sacred Heartbeat Process

The Sacred Heartbeat Process is a simple but powerful meditative exercise by which you can learn to be more in touch with your heart. I like to use this process whenever I feel disconnected from my heart—especially if I have a big decision to make. Coming back to your heart and listening for its guidance can help you to have more clarity and less anxiety in the decisions you make because you are able to tap into your heart's unique intelligence.

Bring your hands to your heart, palms together, and begin to slowly breathe in and out of your heart as you bring in the intention that you are about to touch something very sacred. Like you would gently hold a newborn baby or pet a kitten, this is the energy that your hands send to your heart. Imagine your heart receiving this energy as a child receives a hug, or a lover savors a gentle caress. No matter what challenges are going on in your life, your heart is still beating and emanating its own music. Drink this in and allow yourself to feel the blessing of being alive. Take a few more moments and continue to send loving energy to your heart, allowing this process of giving and receiving to expand.

As you connect more and more with your heart's intelligence, you begin to cultivate your intuition and a "knowing beyond knowing." I define this as the ability to gain access to intelligence and wisdom beyond the boundaries of our thinking minds. You begin to know and understand what is specifically right for you because you are listening to your heart.

Using this process often, we begin to trust our intuition, and in this state of connection our heart becomes the internal advisor and conductor of what resonates with us and benefits us. We spend most of our time sorting through life situations and challenges through our mental process, without the awareness that our heart is constantly serenading us, guiding us, speaking to us; but by using the Sacred Heartbeat Process, you can reconnect with your heart and take its guidance into consideration as well.

Divine Breathing and the Power of the Sigh

If the heart is our internal drummer, the breath is the conductor that leads this internal rhythm section. As we breathe in, we receive our life-force. As we exhale and sigh, we release negative emotions and stress as we empty our vessel. Each breath is a new opportunity to hear and develop a deeper relationship with our inner music. Among this inner music, the sigh is another valuable tool for breathing exercises, as the sigh gives us further control over our breathing, and is part of the internal music we create on a daily basis.

One major benefit of working with the breath is that we can influence our autonomic nervous system in a powerful way. The autonomic nervous system is not under our conscious control, but it has the important job of regulating our bodily functions such as breathing, the heartbeat, and digestive processes. Our breath is one of the biggest influencers of this vital system, which is why it is important to connect to and be aware of our breathing. The following exercise will help you bring awareness to this bodily system and use it to your advantage.

Breathing Exercise

Slowly breathe in. Hold the breath for a moment, and then release it with an audible sigh. Try this several times. Now, bring more of a focus on each breath. As you inhale, visually direct the breath into one area of the body, perhaps to a place where your body currently feels tense or to where you normally hold tension. As you inhale, flex or contract the muscles in that area. As you exhale, let out a powerful sigh and relax that area. Continue doing this throughout your physical body, with particular focus on areas that feel tense or stressed. As you release the sound of the sigh, these areas will begin to feel lighter and less tense.

One of the main reasons we hold so much tension in our bodies is we forget how powerful the breath can be in releasing physical and emotional stress. By pausing and taking one moment to ourselves, we can utilize our breath to "address the stress" and prevent it from escalating into potentially hazardous health issues.

When we practice these breathing techniques, the breath, the sigh, and heart are in constant communication, orchestrating a sense of inner peace. As we release the sigh, not only does our physical body relax, but our mental, emotional, and spiritual bodies relax as well. The sigh is a soul sound that says, *In this moment, everything is all right.* By becoming consciously aware of our heartbeat and our breath, and the use of our sighs, we feel more connected to the peace of the present moment. Our heartbeat, breath, and sigh are our umbilical cord to nourishing a deeper spiritual connection.

Finding Your Unique Heart Code

As we focus more on the interaction of our heart and breath, this focus blossoms to create a deeper understanding and a more intimate relationship with our heart. In addition, we begin to see that there is a unique relationship between our heart and our brain, with each having its own independent intelligence. As we become more familiar with their specific roles, we can shift back and forth based on what is needed in different circumstances. If you over-think situations, experience a lot of mind chatter, second-guess decisions, or are locked into limited belief systems that define you, it's time to give the brain a break.

Your heart is always inviting you to shed the illusion of who you think you are and come home to who you truly are. In the center of you, within your heart, you carry your own unique vibration, your own *heart code*. No one else has the exact vibration that you do. This vibration carries your gifts and your authenticity, the things you are here to share in the world. This is who you truly are. Your heart code is constantly speaking to you, waiting to be deciphered, and you are the only one who can do this. The following exercise that works with the music within—the heartbeat, the breath, and the sigh—will assist you in finding this state of harmony.

Heart Song Breathing Process

Let's incorporate the sacred heartbeat, the divine breath, and the soul sound of the sigh into a powerful process that will allow you to access a more balanced, peaceful state. In this energy you will be more able to tap into the subtle language of your heart and open the door to finding your unique heart code.

This process will incorporate three sacred breaths.

To begin, stand up and gently place your hands on your heart. Spread your feet slightly more than shoulder width apart, as if they are creating the base of a pyramid that points to your heart.

Breath One

As you inhale, visualize bringing the breath in through the bottom of your feet, all the way up your legs, through the hips and abdomen, lower and mid-back, all the way to your heart. As you exhale, visualize releasing this breath out through your heart, and let the breath go with a powerful sigh.

This breath works to clear stresses and stagnant energy held in the lower body, nurturing us through each step we take on our spiritual path. It is imbued with love and appreciation for all that is. It unites us to the energy of Mother Earth that we connect to through the bottom of our feet. Visualize your feet planted and united with the earth, and feel safe and supported.

Breath Two

Now extend your arms above your head and spread them until you create a V shape, as if they were forming an upside-down pyramid that points to your heart. Imagine yourself on top of a beautiful mountain, surrounded by an expansive, unlimited, star-filled sky.

As you breathe in, visualize bringing the breath in through the top of your head, through the brain, face, neck, shoulders, upper back, and chest, and then release your breath through the heart, again with a powerful sigh.

The second breath works to release stresses and stagnant energy held in the upper body, including the mind. This breath asks us to surrender what we cannot control and opens our ability to accept guidance and ask for help. It bonds us to the energy of the Divine Father (often referred to in Native American culture as Father Sky).

Breath Three

The third breath integrates the first two breaths and balances our masculine (Father Sky) and feminine (Mother Earth) energies through the heart. When you inhale with your hands on your heart, visualize this breath coming IN through the heart and OUT through the heart, and release it with a powerful sigh.

Remember, in all three breaths we should be releasing on the exhale with a powerful sigh. The sigh acts as a sound catalyst to release the energy.

After you have tried this three-breath process several times, place your hands on your heart and continue to gently breathe in and out. Hear or feel your heartbeat. Listen to your breath. Let your inner music sing to you. . . . In this relaxed state, allow yourself to simply be.

The Heart Song Breathing Process has been invaluable for me as a type-A native New Yorker involved in the music industry for twenty-five years, helping me manage my daily stresses and form a deeper connection with my heart.

Another benefit of practicing the Heart Song Breathing Process is the calming effect it has on the body. Research has shown that meditations such as these can slow our heart rate, lower blood pressure, increase circulation, aid digestion, strengthen our immune system, improve cognition, and diminish feelings of anxiety, depression, and irritability.

The Heart Song Breathing Process is one of the simplest, most important, and most powerful exercises in this book. It is the first step in appreciating music on a new and different level, by bringing a level of awareness to the music within. Once you are connected to the music within, you will appreciate the external form of music in a new way, one that is beyond art and entertainment, as a fresh and vital tool for transformation.

If this were the only process that you incorporated into your daily music practice, in thirty days it alone would transform you! The following sound tools will assist you in keeping the ideas in this chapter fresh and give you the ability to implement them into your own daily musical program.

Sound Tools for Transformation

1. Listen to the sound of your breath and heartbeat on a daily basis. Honor these sounds as a symbol that you are alive regardless of the challenges you encounter, and give thanks for all you have every day!

2. Make a commitment to place your hands on your heart during or after stressful situations or before a challenging encounter, and simply breathe and connect to your unique vibration.

3. Review the Heart Song Breathing Process in this chapter so that it becomes second nature. Incorporate it into a daily practice. It's a free, noninvasive, fast, and powerful tool to create transformation and a deeper connection with your heart anyplace and anytime!

Suggested Music

This chapter will be one of the few in which there will not be suggested music. Focus on the amazing chorus of sounds within you, and listen on a new level as they begin to speak to and open your heart. As you build this relationship, you will find that your heart begins to speak back, providing hidden wisdom, guidance, intuition, and self-love. All of the answers you have been searching for are here. . . . It's time to listen and come home to the heart!

2

Activating Your Heart's Intelligence with Music

Music is the shorthand of emotion.

—Leo Tolstoy

NOW THAT YOU HAVE LEARNED how to listen to your internal music, let's uncover how the positive emotions that are produced from the techniques used in the last chapter can benefit your mind and body.

The basis of the Heart Song Breathing Process is to move us into a more relaxed state where we become more familiar with our internal sounds—our breath, our sigh, and our heartbeat. This listening creates an understanding that our most basic needs are being met. When we truly listen and can incorporate the wisdom we learn from listening, we begin to cultivate our heart's intelligence. We form a relationship with our heart, and we begin to feel thankful in a simple and powerful way. Thankful for each moment.

Thankful for being alive. Thankful for now. We begin to experience powerful positive emotions such as gratitude, kindness, joy, and love. We know these emotional states can enhance our mental state and our spiritual connection, but they also affect our physical health. Let's look at music's role in taking us there!

Understanding Coherence and Its Role in Health

Coherence occurs when the many aspects of our four bodies (mental, physical, spiritual, and emotional) all come together in harmony to work toward our optimal health. For example, think of the many sections of the orchestra as your body systems. If the violins decided to play at one speed, the flutes at another, and the horns at a third, and all of them were playing whatever notes they wanted, what you would hear would likely be incoherent, fragmented, and dissonant music. There has to be an agreed-upon tempo beforehand, a certain key to play in, and communication between instruments. Each has its individual part to play, but there is a harmony that exists. That is how coherent and synchronized music is made. The heart, as the drummer in the orchestra, has the ability to provide a smooth, steady rhythm that the body can synchronize to. The heart must also communicate to the individual systems (digestive, nervous, etc.) effectively.

Our emotions are the conductor of our orchestra. Research has shown that when we are experiencing positive emotions such as gratitude, kindness, compassion, and joy, we are producing smooth, orderly, synchronized rhythms (coherence). When we are experiencing negative emotions such as anger or frustration, we are producing non-orderly, fragmented rhythms (incoherence).

Positive emotions have also been proven to increase our heart rate variability, which in turn can improve our ability to adapt to physical, emotional, and environmental stresses.[1]

Heart rate variability measures how our heart rhythms change from beat to beat. Imagine that during a piece of music the conductor leads the orchestra to change tempos at various parts of the musical piece. When there is smooth, orderly communication (coherence), the orchestra can adapt to the changes easily. When there is fragmentation, or disjointed communication (incoherence), it is more difficult to adapt to stressful situations and our body and our health pay the price. The more positive and elevated the emotions, the smoother and more orderly the heart rhythms, and the better our heart and other systems can adapt and cope with stress.

The Institute of HeartMath defines coherence in the following way:

> Heart coherence, marked by . . . smooth and balanced heart rhythms, is the optimal state for your heart, mind and emotions and all of the processes in your body, including cognitive, hormonal, digestive, respiratory and immune systems.

The empowering part is that we can have an active role in creating heart coherence and improving our health. As we bring more focus and attention to our heart, we open the path to living a more heart-centered life. Music can be the ultimate mentor in teaching you how to gain access to the doorway of your heart.

The Role of Music in Coherence

Music can play a major role in creating a coherent state because of its effortless power to provide a constant, smooth rhythm and to evoke positive emotions. Our hearts have the ability to adapt and synchronize to the tempo of a piece of music. When the internal rhythm of our heart adapts to the external rhythm of the music, this is called *entrainment*. On average our hearts are at a relaxed state between 60 and 70 beats per minute (bpm). When we listen to soothing, calm music with a beat of around 60 bpm, our heartbeat (internal rhythm) synchronizes to the music (external rhythm) and we can move to a relaxed state. This is part of our heart's unique intelligence, its ability to understand and adapt to the language that music is speaking.

An interesting study has shown that listening to a metronome with a steady beat of 66 bpm can be more effective in reducing anxiety than sitting in silence.[2]

I have applied this same methodology of creating this slower, steady tempo in my own music and have had amazing results in assisting people to reach these coherent states where anxiety is reduced.

One of the benefits of coherence is that when we are in this state, our body is more able to care for and heal itself. The important and powerful bottom line of this is that music can support our bodies to move into this state of repair, detoxification, and rejuvenation. When you combine music with a steady, smooth, orderly rhythm of about 60 bpm, it can create the same results as the metronome study. Even if this rhythm is subtle and underlying, such as in relaxation music, it is amazing that our internal drum (our heart) and our breath can synchronize to external rhythms. This can induce coherent states where our bodies can become more resilient and we are able to adapt to our daily stresses more effectively.

I have testimonials of this in extreme situations, such as delivering a child into the world, where the mother was able to keep her body and mind in a coherent state by adapting her breath to the tempo of my music.

A Newborn's Connection with "The Heart"

Evelyn Simmons, a certified nurse-midwife, reported that at a recent conference she was facilitating for midwives, one of the attendees brought her two-week-old baby who, as expected, was experiencing some fussiness over the course of the two-day convention. During this time, she put on "The Heart" from my CD series *Ambiology* (a piece of music composed at 60 bpm). The facilitator explained that the tempo of this piece of music was designed to create optimal relaxation and entrainment with the heart of both mother and child, and asked the mother to use the vibration and rhythm of the music to connect their hearts. Moments later, while the room was in a deeply relaxed and meditative state, the facilitator noticed something amazing: the baby was no longer fussing! Instead, the child was lying with her belly on her mother's arm, her eyes wide open in wonder and peace. Her arms were moving in sync with the rhythm of the music. When the music was turned off, the baby began to fuss again, but calmed once more almost immediately after the music resumed.

This demonstrates how easily we can entrain our heartbeat to beneficial tempos to promote peace and relaxation. Even the two-week-old infant was able to relax as her heart synced to the rhythm of the music. If entraining the heart with music can help a fussy two-week-old, imagine how helpful this could be in dealing with stress factors in your own life! As our internal clock (our heart) adapts to the external clock (the music), we are gently guided to a state of relaxation. This process of our internal clock synchronizing with an external clock is entrainment in action.

Emotions and Heart Coherence

Like music, emotions carry a specific vibration. When we allow ourselves to experience the energy of gratitude, kindness, compassion, joy, love, and other positive, elevated emotions, our four bodies can move into resonance and harmony with these emotions, which in turn creates more balance in our health and improves our quality of life. These emotions then create a shared, coherent field that is projected from our heart outwardly. I define a shared emotional field as the emotions and energy of an individual being felt beyond him- or herself. We have all experienced this before in one way or another. Imagine you're at an event like the Super Bowl, where you can feel the cumulative energy of all the fans. That energetic feeling is produced by the cumulative emotions of the group. This is a shared field. We can also do this individually.

Have you ever walked into a room with someone and felt that the other person was in a bad mood even before they said anything? We are tapping into their emotions in the shared field. Fortunately, the opposite of this is true. We can tap into positive aspects of the shared field as well.

Music is a powerful tool in creating these shared and individual fields because of its innate ability to carry emotion and intention. For example, if you listen to the same piece of music played by two different musicians, it is likely that one will appeal to you more than the other. This is not because the music itself is any different, but because you are picking up on the musician's emotions and intention *behind* the music. The emotions that come through music create a shared field with the listeners in the same way being at the Super Bowl creates a shared field of excitement.

By listening to specific musical pieces that contain positive emotions, you can create the emotional resonance that you desire, be it peace, gratitude, joy, or exuberance. From this field, you can share those elevated emotions to positively affect yourself and the people in your life, all from carefully choosing and entraining to the music that contains those emotions!

Emotion and intention are the secret ingredients in creating a powerful musical experience. It's like Grandma's meatball recipe.

You can follow the recipe line for line, but something just doesn't taste the same. It's all the love Grandma put into it, seeing and feeling everyone enjoying her meatballs even before anyone ate them. All of that went into the bowl, not just the ingredients. Music is the same. Love is always the secret ingredient!

In addition, research shows that specific types of music can affect our heart health. Classical and meditation music benefit cardiovascular health most, with heavy metal and techno having the least benefit. Blood pressure can also be altered according to the type of music being listened to. Classical music (Mozart) lowered blood pressure, while rock music (Queen) brought blood pressure up.[3]

Taking this to the next level, music can be designed by composers with specific tempos and embedded with positive emotions. The end result is that listeners can benefit by moving from states of stress where their overall heart health is compromised to more positive emotional states where relaxation and rejuvenation occur and health can improve.

The next story shows how this new "designer music" can create a coherent field that others can tap into to also create the beneficial coherent state we have discussed.

Shared Fields and Designer Music

When I set out to write my album *The Heart Codes*, it was with the intention that I would use my insight into heart coherence, music, and entrainment to help others. I wanted this intention to be felt within my music (like an added secret ingredient!), so I created an intention for the start of each specific recording session. For example: "My intention is that the music I am creating assists the listener in forming a deeper connection with their heart." Prior to touching the keyboard, I made sure that my emotions were aligned with my intention, and, if necessary, I would perform the Heart Song Breathing Process to bring my emotions into alignment.

Part of my process is always connecting with the field around me when I create. In this field there are unlimited possibilities, soul-touching melodies, and otherworldly harmonies. A shift occurs in which I move from being the composer to actually being composed in collaboration with a higher power beyond myself. As I become aligned, I tap into the field of all possibilities. I feel warmth in my heart and know when it is time to begin.

While composing *The Heart Codes*, I would begin to play and could feel my heart slow down and entrain to 60 bpm (the tempo my metronome was set to). I felt myself moving to a very relaxed, almost meditative state. I felt completely in sync with the music that was flowing through me. It was almost as if the music was playing me. I felt a strong sense of beauty, peace, and love all around me and within me. That's when I heard a knock on the door, and my fiancée Donese (whose picture should be under the definition of type A) asked me to lower the volume. The music was taking her to a deep state of calm and relaxation, and it was making it difficult for her to work.

I decided to work with my headphones on, but as I moved back into my meditative, relaxed state and the music began to flow through me, I again heard a knock on the door. Even though she couldn't *hear* the music, Donese could *feel* her heart synchronizing to the relaxed and blissful state! I was experiencing coherence through the music that I was creating (as was my intention). My intention aligned with my emotions, harmonics, and frequencies, and it had created a field. This field was being shared with Donese even when she was in another room and could not hear the music!

It felt as though the field that was created from the composition was in harmony with a larger field. After *The Heart Codes* was released, many people told me they felt the music and the emotion in every cell of their body. In this state they were able to form a more intimate relationship with their heart. They experienced the shared field within the music, and it allowed them to reach a more coherent, rejuvenating state. This field was designed by my intention, sparked by the emotion, and carried by the harmonics and the specific frequencies of the music. Thinking about how we can design music to create more coherent states physically, emotionally, mentally, and spiritually is very exciting. What is even more exciting is that by improving our individual states, we affect a larger field around us and have an active role in improving our world!

Each piece of music or each song that helps you transform negative emotions to positive ones takes you one step closer to knowing your heart on a deeper level and tapping into its limitless powers.

In addition to listening to music, taking a more participatory role can also be a great tool for healing. A great example of this is singing. When we sing, we are orchestrating a breathing pattern in conjunction with the singing. It is based on the tempo of the song and the phrases sung. When we sing together, our hearts can entrain to similar patterns and can move to smooth, orderly, coherent heart rhythms and improve heart rate variability.[4]

If you have ever listened to a powerful gospel choir, I am sure you have experienced the shared field of elevated emotions not just in the choir but in the whole church. When you leave in this elevated state, how does it affect the rest of your day and all you come in contact with?

Music is beyond doubt a powerful vehicle that communicates and affects our hearts through our deepest trials and tribulations. Even when the brain is not functioning well, music can communicate to our hearts. In a recent study, Mahler's "Symphony No. 2," an uplifting and high-energy piece, was played to a comatose patient for fourteen days. Although the patient did not come out of the coma, his heart rate variability increased throughout the period when music was played, a sign of overall heart health and of the further adaptability of the heart, even in a patient who was not conscious. So, although the brain was not functioning in its normal state, music still communicated to the heart and improved the overall health of the patient.[5]

The bottom line is that we can utilize music to entrain to more orderly heart rhythms and elevate to more positive emotions. This, in turn, can increase our heart rate variability, which has a host of physical, emotional, and mental benefits:

- Less risk for stress-related illnesses, such as cardiac problems

- Improved cognitive abilities

- Enhanced immune function

- Less anxiety

- A stronger sense of inner peace

It is said that the heart has a mind of its own, yet our heart and brain are in constant communication. The Institute of HeartMath says it beautifully:

> *The heart and brain maintain a continuous two-way dialogue, each influencing the other's functioning. The signals the heart sends to the brain can influence perception, emotional processing and higher cognitive functions. This system and circuitry is viewed by neurocardiology researchers as a "heart brain."*

Now that we've discussed how music engages the heart, in the next chapter we will take a deeper look at how music also engages the brain, resulting in healthier and more coherent physical, mental, emotional, and spiritual bodies.

Sound Tools for Transformation

1. Choose three songs that take you to an elevated emotion: one should embrace the feeling of gratitude, one should embrace the feeling of love, and one should embrace the feeling of joy. Listen to these songs throughout your day when you are stuck in a negative emotion. Work on entraining your heart to these emotional states, and creating a shared field of emotion by listening to (or even singing with) these songs. I have provided three samples below.

2. Utilize the suggested pieces of music below, assisting the heart in entraining to smooth, orderly rhythms. When listening, allow yourself to slow your breath down. You may also wish to place your hands on your heart, which can enhance the experience and bring in a higher emotional and spiritual awareness.

Suggested Music

To induce positive emotions, try listening to these songs:

- For gratitude: "Thank You for This Day" by Karen Drucker.

- For love: "Love Can Build a Bridge" by The Judds.

- For joy: "Joy to the World" by Three Dog Night.

Listening to music at 60 bpm can induce relaxation and heart coherence through entrainment. Here are a few songs to try:

- "Awakening" by Jonathan Goldman—This peaceful soundscape by sound pioneer Jonathan Goldman is filled with beautiful, low, resonant tones surrounded by ethereal voices and textures, which allow the listener to surrender his or her thoughts and journey to the heart effortlessly.

- "Weightless" by Marconi Union—This pulsing blanket of sound and weaving, airy nuances allow you to slow your breath down, release heaviness, and re-center and synchronize to your heart's rhythm.

- "Anointing and Activating" by Barry Goldstein— Take a thirty-minute journey to form a deeper and more intimate relationship with your heart. This song uses specific tones and frequencies that create harmonic coherence and sets the groundwork for a blissfully coherent listening experience.

3

Engaging Your Brain with Music

Music is the medicine of the mind.

—John A. Logan, American soldier and political leader

WE HAVE DISCUSSED IN DETAIL how music works with the heart's intelligence, and the benefits of creating heart coherence; but music can affect more than just our heart. Music can bring similarly spectacular results as a transformative and healing tool for our brain.

Four Ways Music Engages the Brain

The field of music and neuroscience is greatly expanding and is indicating many beneficial ways music can engage and change the brain. Let's discuss music's role in engaging emotion, memory, learning and neuroplasticity, and attention. In looking at the many ways that music engages the brain, we can begin to understand how creating a consistent musical program can target and enhance certain brain functions.

Emotion

Research indicates that music stimulates emotions through specific brain circuits.[6] We can easily see how music engages emotion when a child smiles and begins to dance to a rhythm. He is experiencing the emotion of joy from the music. We also see this when parent and child connect through song. Have you ever listened to a mother singing a lullaby to her newborn baby? It is probably one of the most significant bonding experiences you will ever witness. Outside of it being an emotional experience, it is also a physical experience. One reason for this is a hormone related to bonding called oxytocin. The "cuddle hormone," as it's sometimes called, can be released by singing.[7] No wonder music is such a profound emotional experience for both mother and child!

In addition, research indicates that music assists in producing an array of other beneficial molecules in our biological pharmacy. Listening to music can create peak emotions, which increase the amount of dopamine, a specific neurotransmitter that is produced in the brain and helps control the brain's reward and pleasure centers.[8]

We often feel emotions are experienced from our heart, but an enormous part of emotional stimulus is communicated through the brain. Our newfound understanding of how music engages the brain and heart is leading to innovative ways to utilize music to create emotional understanding. A study from the *Journal of Music Therapy* shows that using songs as a form of communication could increase emotional understanding in autistic children. The study incorporated specific songs to portray different emotions. For example, a composition by Beethoven could be used to represent sadness, or the song "Happy" by Pharrell Williams could be used to represent joy. The children could then indicate and identify emotions based on the songs that represented them. Music succeeded where verbal language failed. Music was able to bridge the brain and heart.[9]

Music evokes and engages our emotions in many stages of our lives both individually and in groups. Music can evoke the deepest emotions and help us process fear, grief, sadness, and resentment, even if these emotions are held on a subconscious level.

Memory

Imagine an elderly man in a wheelchair. His head droops down to his chest, almost in a state of unconsciousness. His name is Henry and, sadly, he is disconnected from the world around him due to severe Alzheimer's. What might reconnect him to the world and improve his awareness?

The movie *Alive Inside* chronicles how music can assist in regaining parts of memory and improve the quality of life of Alzheimer's patients. One of the caretakers in Henry's nursing home interviews his family to find out the type of music Henry used to enjoy listening to before Alzheimer's affected him. By creating playlists incorporating music specifically for Henry, the caretaker helps Henry reconnect with the world around him. His eyes open, he is aware, and he is able to communicate. He was reconnected to his life from the music—his music.

A 2009 study from Petr Janata at the University of California, Davis found that there is a part of the brain that "associates music and memories when we experience emotionally salient episodic memories that are triggered by familiar songs from our personal past."[10] In other words, our own familiar music can reconnect us with deep, meaningful memories from our past, like it did in Henry's case.

These principles are what we will use later to form the basis of specifically constructed playlists to evoke certain emotional responses that we wish to produce.

Learning and Neuroplasticity

Neuroplasticity is the brain's ability to reorganize itself by forming new neural connections throughout life. According to MedicineNet.com, "Neuroplasticity allows the neurons (nerve cells) in the brain to compensate for injury and disease and to adjust their activities in response to new situations or to changes in their environment."[11]

To further clarify, when our brain is damaged, it can find or create new pathways to function properly. Amazingly, music can provide the stimuli to create these new pathways and to help the brain rewire itself in the case of brain injury. For instance, in a groundbreaking study by the University of Newcastle in Australia, popular music was used to assist patients with severe brain injuries in recalling personal memories. The music helped the patients to reconnect to memories they previously could not access.

It's like getting directions to a location. If a road is closed, or you are stuck in traffic, there is sometimes an alternate route to get to the same place. Music can help map that alternate route!

A great example of this is shown in the case of former congresswoman Gabrielle Giffords. Congresswoman Giffords experienced a brain injury as the result of a gunshot wound, which affected her language center and left her almost unable to speak. By engaging her brain through music therapy, singing, and melodic intonation, she was able to provide new information to the brain through music and create a reorganization that helped her to make the connections necessary to relearn language.

This is an extreme case, but many of us have experienced some kind of neuroplasticity in our normal lives. Neuroplasticity, simply put, is our brain's ability to repair connections and find alternate pathways to memories, emotions, and even physical systems such as speech—and utilizing music is a wonderful way to achieve this.

Attention

Ever hear a song that engages you so profoundly it takes hold of your full attention? By engaging our brain and our attention in the right ways, music is able to activate, sustain, and improve our attention.

Using brain images of people listening to short symphonies by an obscure eighteenth-century composer, a research team from the Stanford University School of Medicine investigated the power that music has to hold our attention and showed that peak brain activity occurred during a short period of silence between musical movements—when seemingly nothing was happening. This lead the researchers to theorize that listening to music could help the brain to anticipate events and hold greater attention, just as the listeners demonstrated when they seemed to pay closest attention during the anticipatory silences between musical movements.

My theory is that these silences are indeed part of each composer's intention to guide the listener in interpreting and integrating the music. It is the space between the notes that captivates our full attention and allows the busy mind to communicate and integrate with the heart. It is in these silences, where our focus is total and complete, that true balance and healing can occur, as our brain and heart move into coherence.

On the other hand, we have all experienced how certain types of music can distract us or make us inattentive to tasks at hand. This makes complete sense. Unlike the attentive silences of the previous study, some songs can negatively engage our attention, as we become part of the song's story or scene. Lyrics are descriptive and engage our analytical mind, which could divide our attention.

As we move forward in the following chapters, you will be encouraged to become an expert on using music to access targeted states. You will learn how to use music as a bridge to shift moods, relax, increase your focus, and gain motivation. What's exciting is that you can assist your heart and brain as they move to more balanced and synchronized states using music, sound, and vibration!

Ways to Engage the Brain Using Music

Now that we have seen some of the ways that music engages the brain, let's learn how we can take a role in implementing some of these benefits into active processes.

Play an Instrument

Musical improvisation, which is a spontaneous creative idea, is a perfect example of how music utilizes both sides of the brain. Our technical skills are utilized to play the instrument and affect the left side of the brain, while the new creative ideas or improvisation flowing through us affect the right side. In addition, we are tapping into the power of our hearts by embedding the music with our emotion. On a spiritual level, when I improvise I always feel like the ideas are flowing through me in collaboration and connection with a larger field and something outside myself. If you want to engage both your brain and heart with music, improvise! This practice is not limited to just musicians; I have seen many a friend make up his or her own words to songs on karaoke night!

This skill of improvising can also be applied in different areas of our lives to find creative solutions and improve cognitive abilities and spontaneous thought, which in turn can assist with the challenges we face in our daily lives.

Sing

In addition to singing having beneficial effects for our heart, it also affects our brain as well. Keep in mind that it's about the *act* of singing itself, not how well you sing! Some studies have demonstrated that singing (even bad singing!) provides emotional, social, and cognitive benefits.[12] In addition, in later chapters we will show how music can be used to improve speech function and decrease stress, anxiety, and depression.

Chant

For thousands of years, chanting has been used as a vehicle to form a deeper spiritual connection. This is especially true of the sound *om*, which is said to contain every sound in the universe within it. As we chant *om*, we can release mind chatter and our focus shifts to a deeper spiritual connection. But chanting also benefits our physical body as well as our spiritual one!

A pioneering study revealed that chanting the word *om* could engage the area of the brain that is associated with calmness and a sense of inner peace. fMRIs (functional MRIs) were used to scan the brain while people chanted different sounds and syllables, including *ssss* and *om*. While chanting the sound of *ssss* showed no benefit, chanting *om* activated the area of the brain associated with a sense of peacefulness.[13]

Drum

Research indicates that specific beats can induce different brain wave frequencies and can induce a deeply relaxed state.[14] Other studies show that participation in group drumming led to significant improvements in many aspects of social-emotional behavior.[15]

The potential of the benefits of drumming on the brain is leading to some amazing collaborations. Mickey Hart, former drummer of the Grateful Dead, paired with neuroscientist Dr. Adam Gazzaley in hopes of gaining a deeper understanding of how music directly affects different brain wave states and how it may help specific brain conditions. Dr. Gazzaley measured Hart's brain wave activity as he played at concerts. Hart led a drum circle of over a thousand people.

It demonstrated the natural power of group rhythmic entrainment, and their findings supported recent studies that indicated how playing a musical instrument can strengthen and exercise the aging brain. We'll discuss the benefits of drumming more later on.

Brain Wave Entrainment

Another powerful way to engage the brain with music, sound, and vibration is through brain wave entrainment. Although this section gets a bit heady (excuse the pun), I invite you to stick with me and embrace your inner geek.

Heart entrainment, discussed in the previous chapter, shows how the internal rhythm of our heart can synchronize to the external rhythm of music to create more orderly, beneficial heart rhythms. But music can also entrain the brain to more relaxed states, where we become more focused and attentive and can increase our cognitive abilities, sleep more soundly, and learn to meditate.

While heart entrainment is based upon synchronizing the heartbeat to specific tempos, or beats per minute, brain entrainment is based on the brain synchronizing to specific frequencies, which are measured in hertz (Hz).

Specific frequencies induce different states in our brain:

Wave Name	Hertz (Hz) Levels	Effect	Example
Beta waves	14–40 Hz	Awake, normal alert consciousness	Actively conversing or engaging in work
Alpha waves	8–14 Hz	Calm, relaxed	Meditating, reflecting, taking a break from work
Theta waves	4–8 Hz	Deep relaxation and meditation, mental imagery	Daydreaming
Delta waves	0–4 Hz	Deep, dreamless sleep	Experiencing REM sleep

During our active day most of us are in beta states. We are moving at a faster pace when our attention is on our outer world (work, family, etc.), and our faster brain frequencies reflect this. As we move to more relaxed brain wave states, we become calmer. We can induce the alpha state by closing our eyes, breathing slower, and listening to calming music.

As we travel into an even deeper state of relaxation, we move into a theta brain wave state. This can occur through meditation and also through relaxation music. It is in alpha and theta states that we tap into enhanced creative frames of mind. As our bodies progress into deep sleep, we are in delta and our brain waves have fully slowed down.

Music is a delivery system of frequency. Each note has a specific frequency, but we can also embed additional brain wave frequencies outside of the standard notes into music to allow the brain to entrain to our desired states.

When our internal brain waves synchronize to the external brain wave frequencies that are contained in the music, this is called brain wave entrainment. For instance, if I were looking to move into a very creative state, I would utilize music that contains alpha and theta frequencies. If I have insomnia, I might incorporate music that contains delta frequencies.

There are many technologies that are used to induce and target the different brain frequencies, including binaural beats, isochronic beats, monaural beats, and many more. Each type could have its own chapter. I invite you to investigate the pros and cons of them all and see which ones resonate with you. In addition, I am creating my own delivery system called adaptive music, which utilizes specific harmonics to accommodate the different targeted brain states.

An amazing amount of research has been done to prove the benefits of music on the brain, but we've only just scratched the surface. There is so much excitement and potential around integrating music as a transformative pathway to heal and improve our brains. I am thrilled to be working with Dr. Daniel Amen, who is a double board-certified adult and child psychiatrist, author, and researcher. We will be conducting exciting new research to determine how my music may provide supportive benefits to the brain and to determine how to create and influence positive changes by selecting specific pieces of music to improve brain function.

I have also had the privilege of working with Dr. Joe Dispenza, a researcher, lecturer, and author, and have composed live music to accompany his meditations with over five hundred attendees at each workshop. During these powerful meditations, a group of participants was studied using EEG brain mapping technology to determine specific brain activity. The research showed people reached very coherent brain wave states in a very short period of time during the meditations. It is amazing to see firsthand how music and meditation can help in moving people to beneficial brain states where transformation can occur.

Knowing how to entrain both our hearts *and* our brains can lead us to a place of true synchronization, where our heart and mind are seamlessly connected in constant communication through the music we listen to.

At the end of the chapter, I have provided examples of the types of music that induce the different brain wave states to help you get started on your journey toward your own brain entrainment exercises! As you become more familiar with the frequencies that evoke specific responses within your brain, you should feel free to branch out and find other pieces of music that can help you achieve these brain wave states.

Imagine being able to utilize the power of both your brain and heart for transformation and healing. All it takes is choosing the right set of music . . .

Sound Tools for Transformation

The suggested music below incorporates different targeted brain wave states. Review the brain wave chart in this chapter and select one of the pieces below to move you to the brain state of your choice.

- Listen to a piece of music that brings you to a highly elevated and inspired emotional state. I love to listen to powerful instrumental music like that of Vangelis or epic soundtrack music. Moving to this brain state creates the potential for the production of beneficial hormones, neurotransmitters, and other molecules in your body. For example, after listening to music, serotonin levels can increase. Serotonin is involved in the sleep-wake cycle, mood, and the control of pain perception.

- Choose a piece of familiar music to engage your memory. Find a song that takes you back to an event that engages positive emotions. Notice how the brain not only remembers the music, but also the original emotion. Use this powerful tool on a daily basis!

Suggested Music

- "Wisdom of the Heart" by Barry Goldstein—A beautiful one-hour musical journey that gently entrains the heart and brain to a more relaxed, coherent state. Transcend from your "type A" beta days to peaceful alpha nights!

- "Deep Theta 2.0 Part 1" by Steven Halpern—Allow the trance-inducing shakuhachi bamboo flutes and the legendary signature Rhodes electric piano of Steven Halpern transport you into a deep theta brain wave state.

- "Delta Sleep System Part 1" by Dr. Jeffrey Thompson—A wonderful tapestry of lush sound and minimal melodies creates the perfect foundation to assist with sleeping challenges or winding down before bedtime.

4

Song as a Vehicle
for Transformation

Music is the divine way to tell beautiful,
poetic things to the heart.

—Pablo Casals

I CAN STILL HEAR MY FATHER SINGING in the car as "Maggie
Mae" by Rod Stewart blasts through the black Cadillac's speakers.
My dad was a limousine driver for eighteen hours a day, six days a
week for over twenty years. It's hard to imagine how many hours of
music he listened to in a day to shift his mood, to keep him awake,
to allow him to nap for an hour. I can still hear his voice saying with
his slightly Jewish New York accent, "Now *that's* a song! When are
you gonna write a song like that?"

He especially loved the line in Maggie Mae that referred to
the character stealing his father's pool stick and skipping school. I
could feel his emotions in the moment where he proudly sang that

line louder than the others. It always took him from his limousine back in time to that pool hall in Brooklyn where he spent many hours not only learning the game of pool but the game of life.

I can almost smell the cigarettes in his car ashtray, the day-old coffee cups in the holder, and the leather interior, mixing with Rod Stewart's voice and my dad's. I am there, right now in the limousine, and although my dad has passed on, he will always live in that song for me. "Maggie Mae," courtesy of Rod Stewart, transformed my dad every time he heard it, providing about four minutes of joy in a long eighteen-hour day. For a few moments in that song, he was given a vehicle that transported him to a different space and time. All was still good in that pool hall, surrounded by the love of his childhood buddies and the piece of him that wished he could play hooky from those eighteen-hour days six days a week, fifty-one weeks a year. It may seem small, but there are no small transformations; they are all miracles.

Music defies time and embraces space. Just as it did for my dad, music takes us all back to grade school in an instant, to our first breakup, or to our walk down the aisle. Songs give definition to our emotions and create the soundtrack of our lives. Music allows us a brief intermission in challenging times. This intermission allows our souls to rest, recuperate, and recharge our hearts. A song may be just as powerful as a favorite movie or book that changed your worldview.

The Messenger: Song

A song can be a long-lost friend. Although you may not have communicated with it in years, when you do listen, it instantly transports you to another place and time and evokes strong emotions. Song is a vehicle for the soul to release burdens and heavy energy. Creating movement to release our negative emotions sets the space for a shift to occur. These shifts in feelings can release emotional blocks, which in turn aid in our healing process. When we alter our emotions, there can be a profound effect on the physical body. When we create a change in any of the four bodies—physical, emotional, mental, or spiritual—we are creating movement in at least one of the others. Songs move emotions, period.

Let me give you an example. Think of a song like "Eleanor Rigby" by The Beatles. In this hauntingly beautiful two-minute song, John Lennon and Paul McCartney take you through the lives of two lonely people, including a wedding and a funeral. The lives of these two people intertwine within the song, although we are not sure if they have ever physically met.

Although we, as the listener, have never met them either, by the time the song is over we feel as though we know them through the amazing development of the characters. There is a "common chord" (excuse the pun) being struck within all of us. The haunting cellos and moving violins pull at our heartstrings and open our hearts. For less than three minutes we are in this song's scene, feeling the sadness and loneliness of the characters. This gives us a platform to acknowledge our own challenges with loneliness, and to use the compassion the song activates toward ourselves. It creates an opportunity to heal.

When we hear a song that resonates with us, it is amplifying something within us that is already there and may need to be brought to the surface to explore, understand, and release from our heart. The song is a messenger from the soul, bringing awareness to these hidden emotions and blockages.

Have you ever had a song come on at the perfect moment? These are soul messages that are inviting you to listen more deeply to what truths your spirit is trying to convey.

I remember going through a challenging time in my life, and whenever I was questioning my faith, "Angel" by Sarah McLachlan would come on. I remember the comfort in those moments of knowing I was held and comforted by something outside of myself that I could not explain. That song was my soul's messenger that everything was going to be okay . . . I believed it and felt it, and it was.

Another song came as a message to my soul when I met my fiancée. For years, whenever someone would ask me what my favorite song was, I would answer, "Could It Be I'm Falling in Love" by The Spinners. It was a song that brought me back to a very happy time in my childhood. But in all my years as a musician and songwriter, I have never had one person tell me that this was their favorite song.

One night, early on in our relationship, Donese and I were having a conversation on the phone and I asked her what her favorite song was. When she answered "Could It Be I'm Falling in Love" by The Spinners, I nearly fell off my chair. I didn't think she would believe me when I told her it was my favorite song as well. In that moment, it was a message to both of us that this obscure 1970s record was a sign that we were two pieces of a puzzle meant to fit together.

In addition to being the soul's messenger, song has also been used as a messenger between individuals and groups of people.

African American slaves used music to boost their spirit individually and in groups, and certain songs also became a way to relay secret messages. "Wade in the Water," for instance, contains messages of how to avoid bloodhounds. Another song, "Follow the Drinking Gourd," provided details to slaves of an escape route from Mississippi and Alabama to Canada.[16]

In these examples, music was not only used as a soul messenger to keep spirits and hopes alive, but also as a powerful interpersonal messenger—one that helped to save lives.

Songs move us beyond the mind and take us directly to the core of our soul. At this deep level we can transmute and transform limited beliefs and negative feelings and emotions. As we clean out emotions from our energetic closet that no longer serve us, we can begin to truly listen to our heart and unveil the gifts that we are here to share. We all have a song in our heart that is waiting to be sung.

Orchestrating Your Heart's Song in This Moment

In 2004, I was captivated by Dr. Wayne Dyer's talk at a conference in Arizona. I still remember the eight words he said: "Don't die with your music still in you." *Wow*. It went straight to my heart. While I was working at producing and collaborating on other people's music every day, I put aside writing and singing my own songs. Every time I would begin to sing my music, I would hear the voices of my childhood buddies saying, "Dude, don't sing." I listened to those naysaying voices for over twenty years.

I decided in that moment of hearing Wayne Dyer speak, seemingly directly to me, that I was done listening to those negative voices. I made a commitment to write, sing, and produce my first solo album. I didn't care if one person listened to it; I was not about to die with my music still in me.

I released my first solo album at the age of forty-four. In honor of the moment that I committed to it, I called it *The Moment*. One year later, through a series of synchronicities, and my tenacious and heart-connected events manager Sharon Kelley, I was asked to open up for Wayne Dyer in Colorado. I sang the title song, "The Moment." After my performance, he affectionately rubbed the top of my head in approval and it felt as though my dad were blessing me from the other side, saying, *Son, I am proud of you!*

Inspiration creates inspiration. Once I released that limiting belief system of "Dude, don't sing," I was supported by each step I took in moving forward. Small steps create large movement, and the universe blatantly responded. At that time, I did not know Wayne and he did not know me, but here was an alignment that was occurring, a harmony that the universe, Wayne, and I were now creating together to benefit each person who listened.

Is there something lying dormant in you, waiting to be sung? It does not have to be a literal song. Maybe it's something that you are waiting to share in the world or have put on hold. The world needs you now; it needs your gifts, and it needs your heart's song. Your heart's song is a vibration or purpose you carry in your heart that is waiting to be shared.

Take a moment and find a quiet place. Make sure there are no distractions. Take a minute to review the Heart Song Breathing Process from chapter one. Allow yourself time to connect with your inner music, your heartbeat, and your breath. Awaken what is dormant in you by shining the light of awareness on it!

In the following chapters, we will delve deeper into how you can personally use song in your everyday life to create the kinds of transformation you want to see. Just as I did when I heard Wayne Dyer speak (hearing him in my heart as well as with my ears), you will be able to release old patterns and ideas that you have engrained into your brain and heart and receive the messages from your soul, encouraging and guiding you to explore, expand, and create in ways that are fulfilling and satisfying. You are the conductor of the orchestra of your life; all it takes is the commitment to put your practices into action to effect the changes you desire.

Sound Tools for Transformation

Is it possible that you are being guided to a message through song? Take a moment to answer the following questions:

- Have you recently heard several songs that have a common subject or theme?

- Has there been a particular song that really resonates with you that you find yourself listening to multiple times?

- Could this song relate to a specific situation in your life that you have been challenged by?

- What is the message to your soul that this song conveys?

- Is it possible to use this message to transform the energy of the situation?

- Is there a song that you have listened to that comforts you? Inspires you?

- What is lying dormant in you, just waiting to be awakened? Is there something you have put on hold that your heart is longing to share?

- What steps can you take right now, in this moment, to begin to share your heart's song?

These questions and answers may bring light to an issue or situation that is just waiting to be transformed. If your answers lead you to feeling called to listen to a particular song, take a moment to give that to yourself.

Suggested Music

"Your Song" by Elton John—I was nine years old when I first heard this song, and it still touches me to this day. This classic pop song written by Elton John and Bernie Taupin truly captures the ability of a simple song to tap into the beauty of life. As the lyrics imply, we all can have a song that sheds light on how wonderful life is and can be. Incorporate it somewhere in your day and let the delicate piano and gentle melodies serenade your heart!

PART TWO

Creating *and* Implementing *a* Daily Music Practice

5

Music: The Bridge to Re-tuning Emotions

I was born with music inside me. . . . Music was one of my parts.
Like my ribs, my liver, my kidneys, my heart. Like my blood.
It was a force already within me when I arrived on the scene.
It was a necessity for me—like food or water.

—Ray Charles

MY DAD AND MOM WERE MUSIC LOVERS. We had a ton of 45s and 33s (which were called records for those of you under forty) in a variety of styles and genres. My dad even worked for Mercury Records at one time. Although they encouraged me musically, the common chorus in my house was, "Music's a nice hobby, but what are you going to do for a living?" When a verbal event is repeated frequently and is attached to an emotion, we begin to absorb it into our field and it creates its own frequency. This frequency, when repeated enough times, creates a vibration, or a belief system, centered around the original words.

For years I carried my parents' belief that music was a nice hobby but it would not sustain me financially. There was a part of me that did not believe in myself 100 percent because subconsciously I did not believe my parents did. The truth is that they were passing on limited belief systems about lack of money and poverty that were passed down to them. I had fallen out of tune.

Specific negative emotions can trigger limited belief systems, just as striking a tuning fork can induce a piano to vibrate when it resonates with the same note. In my case, situations that involved the energy of lack triggered or induced emotions connected to my limited belief system that I was not capable of making a living doing music. This subconsciously sabotaged my ability to move forward with embracing music as a full-time career. When I finally became aware of this, I was able to make the decision that this inherited belief system needed to stop.

It was time to shift the belief system and attune to a new vibration—and I had the perfect tool: music! I immersed myself in the songs of other musicians who had overcome their obstacles to create success. Every time I listened to one of their songs, it became a vehicle to charge my passion and shift my limited beliefs. One of my favorites was Bruce Springsteen, who, like me, had grown up in a working-class neighborhood in the tristate area on the East Coast.

Utilizing the power of song and experiencing musical successes allowed me to overcome my old patterning. What I realized was that creating music was not about making a living; it was a powerful vehicle to assist me in creating an amazing life—the life that I wanted for myself. Once I achieved this amazing life through music, the money naturally followed.

Re-tuning Old Belief Systems

Our belief systems are similar to a piano. Just as pianos can go out of tune and then be re-tuned, so can our belief systems. For example, if a piano has not been tuned in a long time, it becomes accustomed to being de-tuned. The tension of the strings has changed, the relationship of the notes to each other is not optimal, and the overtones are not harmonious. When we finally tune the piano back to its optimal tuning, it tends to shift back to the old tension of being de-tuned. It is used to being this way, and there is literally a pull to return to the old way. We have all experienced the same sensation of de-tuning, or falling out of alignment, and the pull of returning to our limited belief systems.

Most of us come into the world connected and tuned to elevated emotions such as love, appreciation, gratitude, and worthiness. Repetitive events trigger lower vibrational or negative emotions such as shame, guilt, resentment, etc., and we become de-tuned from the elevated emotions contained in our original birth blueprint. Just like the piano, we can grow accustomed to not being tuned properly. It becomes comfortable, and we forget our true potential or our optimal tuning.

So how can we re-tune and maintain without falling back into old patterns and limited belief systems? An excellent way to achieve this is by implementing songs on a daily basis, which can keep us in tune and tapped into our fullest potential.

By frequently listening to a song with elevated emotions, you can shift your negative emotions and limited belief system. The key is being present, truly feeling and becoming the emotion in the song and using it as a consistent daily tool.

Identifying Your Musical Pinnacle

Music can never be taken away from us because it is embedded in us. As Ray Charles said, music is a necessity. Even if we are not listening to music out loud, our brain remembers it and can access it. Right now, if I want to listen to "ABC" by The Jackson 5, I can hear it in my mind. Not only can I hear it, I can also feel it and it can transform my current emotional state.

We all have a song in our memory banks that triggers joy. Some call it a "happy song"; I call it a *musical pinnacle*. It is a song that defines a specific period in your life that you can go back to in an instant and feel the same emotion, usually a time when you were happy. As we discussed before, music cuts through space and time, and transports us to the moment or emotional memory we wish to obtain. Your musical pinnacle acts as a time machine to that specific emotional memory, and it ignites positive emotions in your heart's electromagnetic field and can produce beneficial hormones, chemicals, and molecules from your brain. An example of this would be that when we are experiencing intense pleasure from listening to music, it can lead to the release of dopamine.[17] Dopamine has a number of roles and functions in movement, memory, cognition, and behavior, and it helps control our brain's reward and pleasure centers.

Just like Henry, the Alzheimer's patient, your musical pinnacle might be a lifeline for you in a later period in your life. For Henry, music improved his life by bringing him to an alive-aware state from a completely disconnected one. Music was a life-sparking bridge that transformed his state. Your musical pinnacle, or your "happy song," isn't just a way to create a momentary shift; it is an investment in your future health. As you practice with this song further and further, adding additional layers of happy or joyful emotional memories, it will become easier and easier to reconnect with this song anytime you feel unhappy, disconnected, or out of touch.

Be the DJ of Your Life

When you really take the time to understand the role of a great DJ, what they do can be truly amazing. They understand the power of a five-minute song, and ultimately they can utilize these songs to create an energetic musical map to unforgettable events. Think about the music at a wedding reception. When you come into the cocktail hour, the music is all about creating a safe, inviting space. It's usually more intimate, with just acoustic guitar or piano music. Most of the time the music is instrumental, which gives the guests an opportunity to talk and get to know each other without having to shout over song lyrics. The tempo of the music is either mid or slow tempos to allow the guests to begin to relax and get accustomed to the environment.

As you move into the reception area, the music changes and the acoustic instrumentals are replaced by full songs. Drums, bass, saxophone, and vocals now fill the space and bring energy, excitement, and fun. The music is a bit louder and faster and feels like it is preparing you for something. During dinner, the music is at a lower volume and allows you to socialize but still continues to create a feel-good flow.

After dinner, the master of ceremonies asks for the bride and her father to grace the dance floor with the first dance. They dance to the song, and the bride gently takes a tissue to her father's eye to wipe away a tear. There is not a dry eye in the house. When the dance is over, the groom taps the father of the bride on the shoulder to cut in. The DJ starts playing the song "Celebration" by Kool & The Gang, and everybody is up and going crazy. For the next hour the music gets louder, faster, and more exciting as it creates a climax to an amazing event.

In just a few hours, you were relaxed, emotionally touched, and excited. In addition, your physical body was affected at all of the stages. Music played a powerful and primary role in creating the energetic map for your journey. This was no accident. The DJ knew exactly what songs would work at what times. Imagine taking some of the same principles and applying them to your own life to create an energetic road map to amazing events every day!

So now it's your turn to become the DJ of your life. Our first step to using music as a vehicle is to map out where you want to go and how to get there.

Playlist Protocols

For our purposes, a playlist is a compilation of songs you put together to create a specific mood, emotion, or energetic outcome. Before MP3s, before CDs, there were jukeboxes where we put in coins and picked records we wanted to hear to create a mood. Now we have the ability to download songs, import them into our library, and create mixes by simply dragging them into a new playlist. If this is sounding foreign to you and you are a bit more old-school, you can create your list with pen and paper and play the songs on your list from your CDs or records, eight-tracks, or cassette tapes.

There are a few things to consider that will enhance your listening experience and help you in bringing awareness to your musical preferences, which determines your experience. These tips will also help you begin to differentiate between hearing and *listening*. When we hear something we are merely having a sonic experience. When we listen, we open ourselves up to being affected on a mental, emotional, physical, and spiritual multisensory adventure.

Volume

How loud you listen to music plays a major role in determining your experience in all types of music. Find a comfortable listening level based on the experience you are looking to have according to your playlist.

For relaxing music, I recommend listening at low volumes to encourage a relaxation response.

Volume for your inspirational playlist will differ from your relaxation list. In this case, you might want to get up and dance and really feel the music. The music might be a little louder to accommodate that. It's all about what feels good to you. Find your comfort zone. Obviously, if disturbing others is a concern, consider listening with headphones or inviting them to join in.

Tempo

Tempo is the speed at which a song is played and is related to bpm, or beats per minute. We discussed bpm and tempo at length in our discussion of heart entrainment; now it's time to put that knowledge to good use!

What is the energetic flow you want to create in your playlist? If you are using a playlist to start your day, you might want it to go from slow to fast so you can ease into the experience and then create more energetic movement. If you are making a playlist for the end of the day, the reverse might be true: you want to move the music from faster to slower tempos. If you are listening to a playlist in the middle of the day to relieve stress and calm down, you might want the tempo to be consistent, staying at the same bpm. In general, slow songs are usually between 40 and 70 bpm. Medium tempo songs are between 75 and 115 bpm, and fast songs are 120 bpm and up. If you want to find out the bpm of a song, you can go to www.tempotap.com. Tap along with any song using the space bar to find the bpm!

Genre

When you are compiling songs for your playlists, ask yourself if the genre is conducive to the intention of the playlist. If you are creating a relaxation playlist, most of us will not choose heavy metal music for this purpose. Go through your current library of music—many times the genres are listed if you are using iTunes. If not, YouTube has playlists for many different genres. Listen to and familiarize yourself with the different feel of each genre so you can create a guideline of how to utilize them in your playlists. This will also better acquaint you with genres that you normally don't listen to but might enjoy. Push yourself out of the box a bit and make it a fun adventure.

Rhythm

Rhythm is a repeated pattern of movement or sound accented by short and long notes. The rhythmical accents can evoke a certain mood. If you are creating a sensual playlist, using a slow salsa rhythm or Afro-Cuban rhythm can be quite effective because they are very dynamic. If you are creating an exercise playlist, club or dance music, with its steady, driving rhythm, can motivate your movement. If you are looking for music for a romantic dinner, the smooth rhythm in your favorite jazz album might work wonderfully. Experiment, listen to different rhythms of musical pieces that you love, and see what moods are evoked. Take notes so you can come back and incorporate the themes into your specific playlists. You can use many genres with different rhythms all in one playlist to evoke a targeted emotion.

Melody

Remember the game show "Name That Tune"? What people were using to correctly guess the name of the song was the melody. Melody is the part of the song you can hum or whistle even without the words.

"Beat It" by Michael Jackson is a perfect example of how a melody can continue to be resonant with people years after the song is originally released. DJs still play that song to get people out of their seats thirty years later because the melodic pattern from the bass line is programmed in most of our subconscious memories and makes us feel good. Some other great examples are "Rock Around the Clock" by Bill Haley & His Comets, "Sweet Caroline" from Neil Diamond, "Piano Man" by Billy Joel, or "Shake It Off" by Taylor Swift.

There are times when we might not necessarily want a lot of melody in a musical piece. Music for sleep is one example. When listening to sleep music, we don't want a lot of melody because it can tend to put us into our analytical mind of "I like that melody" or "I don't like that melody." Simple, longer tones with less melody work much better to wind us down, and they don't create what I call earworms (a song that won't leave your mind). Think about the theme song from *Jeopardy*—that is an earworm! Now try to get it out of your mind. . . .

Lyrics

Lyrics are the words in a song. When creating your playlists, consider whether you want songs with lyrics or not. Typically, in relaxation music, full lyrical content that tells a specific story can be distracting, although chanting, which has fewer words and more sounds, can be very conducive to eliciting a relaxation response. Words carry energy, and we listen to songs with words in a more active way because we feel the need to decipher their meaning.

Lyrics can also trigger specific emotions. Sometimes lyrics can inspire and ignite us or bring us to tears. They also can create a multisensory experience. As we tap into the scenes within the song's words, they evoke our senses. Sometimes repeating lyrics can help reprogram and clear negative emotions, and sometimes they can take us to a very vulnerable state. Make sure you use lyrics to take you to your intended state, rather than one you're not ready to explore. As you're composing your playlists, take a minute to look up or listen closely to the lyrics in the songs so you won't be triggered by a phrase that takes you to an unintended emotional state.

Frequencies

As a music producer, I always think creating a song is like building a house out of frequencies. The lower frequencies, bass and low drums, create the foundation for the house. They are the lowest part of the house, usually the part that connects to the earth. Your mid frequencies are like the walls of the house. Guitars, keyboards, synthesizers, and vocals start in this range. Your high frequencies are like the roof of the house. They are shakers, cymbals, and the higher end of the vocal and guitar range.

These frequencies can also work in a beneficial way and have a spiritual context. The lower tones tend to ground us, so if you are feeling scattered or unfocused, listening to music that has a good amount of bass can make you feel more present. Midrange instruments, such as the hand drums in Native American cultures, are used to clear energy around the body. Listening to higher frequencies tends to connect us more with the ethereal, and breathy tones are great for clearing mind chatter and opening up our intuition and spiritual connection. As we discussed in chapter 3, utilizing specific frequencies can help you induce and entrain to particular brain states. Use the brain waves chart in chapter 3 as a quick reference guide for embedded frequencies.

Chords/Modes

When we play different notes together they create chords. Different chords, or modes, can create different emotional experiences. Minor chords can make you feel sad, contemplative, and retrospective, while major chords can make you feel happy, confident, and inspired. Here are some basic emotions that are associated with different chords or modes:

- Major chords—confident, happy, elevated, inspired, extraverted

- Minor chords—sad, somber, introspective

- Diminished chords—ominous, haunting, spooky

- Suspended chords—tense, anticipatory

- Augmented 9th chords—dramatic, very present

- Major 7th chords—dreamy, sensual

You probably have experienced all of the above listed modes, although you may not know the particular names of the chords that were played. You really don't need to. Listen to the feelings that the music evokes in you and see if it is steering you in the direction you want to go.

Keeping these playlist protocols in mind will help as you begin to design new playlists. When we can truly listen to the music within, as discussed in chapter 1, it deepens our experience of recorded and live music. When the external music resonates with the internal music (the heartbeat, the breath, and the sigh), the seed of transformation is nurtured. Listening can be an adventure; and where adventure is invited, transformation awaits!

Sound Tools for Transformation

Here are some powerful suggestions for implementing some of this chapter's concepts to create transformation in your life right now.

- Is there a belief system that has been holding you back from something? Write it down. If you were a doctor, what would be the one song you would prescribe to yourself today to assist you in reprogramming that belief?

- Looking at your schedule tomorrow, become the DJ of your day! What songs can guide you toward the energy you need during different situations in your day?

- Find a song from another culture that moves you. Close your eyes and create a five-minute vacation, allowing the music to transport you to that culture. See the beauty, smell the smells, taste the foods. I have also suggested a song below.

- Practice using your musical pinnacle, or "happy song," throughout your day to invite the emotion of joy whenever you need a pick-me-up. Hum, sing, or simply tap out the beat to reconnect with your memories of happiness and allow it to shift you into an elevated and positive state.

Suggested Music

"La Isla Bonita" by Madonna—The relaxing rhythms and gentle world melodies transport you to a beautiful tropical island in under five minutes. The perfect song to take a virtual vacation to!

6

Creating Playlists for Transformation

*Music... takes us out of the actual & whispers
to us dim secrets that startle our wonder
as to who we are & for what, whence & whereto.*

—Ralph Waldo Emerson

WHEN I WAS ABOUT EIGHT YEARS OLD, my parents moved my sister and I up to the Bronx. We were living in a quiet section of Queens at the time, and our neighborhood was primarily Jewish. Co-op City in the Bronx was conversely a melting pot of all cultures. With thirty-five buildings in a two-and-a-half-mile radius, it was quite different from Queens. By the time I was twelve, I had started playing guitar and writing songs about *everything*. My friends were pretty supportive, but I was teased a bit about creating "musical records" of some not-so-proud moments in their lives. (A song about stealing a school bus could be a bit incriminating.)

I learned early that songs were a way to immortalize significant events, life lessons, and special moments. I began to listen to some great songwriters of the time such as Elton John, The Rolling Stones, and many more. What was truly amazing was that our neighborhood park, which we called Pebble Lounge, became the sounding board for my friends and I to stick our toes into the diverse musical waters surrounding us. With Joe's boom box by our side, each of us would have about a half hour to share a mixtape of our favorite songs. Mixtapes were our playlists in the 1970s. Spending an evening at Pebble Lounge was like tasting from a smorgasbord of music. Everything from salsa by Tito Puente and Celia Cruz to Crosby, Stills & Nash, The Grateful Dead, The Doors, Elvis Costello, The Sugarhill Gang, Bruce Springsteen, Bob Marley, and so many more. The ethnic diversity of growing up in Co-op City provided me with music lessons that could not be taught in a classroom.

Every mixtape came with explanations and insights from the person who created it. It was incredible how every song had its own effect on each of us. Sometimes they affected us differently, sometimes similarly; but the songs always took us somewhere.

Music for us was more than just an escape. In some instances, music acted as a coping mechanism for some very difficult situations that were going on in our families. Music was a way to feel and vent every emotion from anger to love without harming anyone. Listening to our mixtapes was a way to lighten the emotional load that each of us was carrying, and really one of the only tools outside of sports that we had at that time as kids.

It was in these moments, exploring music at Pebble Lounge, that I learned music is a vehicle that can take us from one place to another, from dark to light, transforming us as we travel.

Although mixtapes have now shifted to playlists, the concept is still the same. In this chapter, we will create playlists that take us to specific positive emotions or moods. I usually start with six basic categories—gratitude, inspiration, joy, motivation, peace, and relaxation—but use your creativity to expand these on your own. Once you get this down, you can create playlists for virtually anything: a day at the beach, songs for rainy days, or a great playlist for exercise.

In addition, a sample playlist can be found in the back of the book for the categories mentioned based on my personal experience. See what resonates with you. And remember, when something resonates with you, it amplifies a vibration that already exists in you. This is all part of a more subtle listening experience.

What I love about the process of listening to other people's playlists is that I get turned on to some great music I've never heard before! I love the musical adventure. I also get to understand the other person on a deeper level through the music they've selected.

The genres that you use for the songs in the playlists listed are really up to you. For example, in my gratitude playlist I have a Karen Drucker song called "Thank You for This Day." It is very earthy with a world influence and is mid-tempo. In the same playlist I have "Thank You (Falettinme Be Mice Elf Agin)" by Sly and the Family Stone. It is very funky R&B and it is up-tempo. Remember . . . you are orchestrating your experience, so feel free to mix it up as much as you like!

Bridging Emotional States with Playlists

Each time you listen to a piece of music, you unleash the potential to take a powerful journey. Just as embarking on a trip to an unknown place can evoke an array of emotions—excitement, fun, peacefulness—one song, when used with intention and awareness, can be just as powerful. The main difference is a song can do it in five minutes or less and, on average, costs only about a dollar. Just as a bridge takes you from one side to another, music can become the bridge that takes you from one emotional state to another.

When we group songs that all have a similar intention or are geared toward evoking a positive emotion, it can amplify the experience. This is where playlists shift from just being a concept in iTunes to becoming a powerful vehicle to programing your life!

Identify Contracted and Expansive Energetic States

Before you create a playlist, it is important to identify what energetic state you are presently in, what energetic state you want to go to, and what music playlist you can use as the bridge to take you there.

Many times, we are so caught up in our life situations that we are unaware of our present energetic condition. Whenever I feel a bit out of balance or like something is not quite right, I always check in and ask myself, "Do I feel like I am in a contracted energetic state or an expansive energetic state?"

A *contracted* energetic state is one in which:

- Our energy feels pulled in, as if it were a cold winter day and we are shivering.

- Our muscles feel tight.

- We are stressed.

- We question our gifts and our soul's purpose.

- We feel disconnected.

- Something or someone has triggered us emotionally.

- We feel small, with limited possibilities.

- We are in a place where ego is in charge.

- We are not listening to our intuition.

- We are playing the victim.

An *expansive* energetic state is one in which:

- Our energy feels far-reaching and widespread, like being under a beautiful night sky with our arms held open.

- We feel relaxed and at peace or inspired and motivated.

- We trust in our reason for being here.

- We feel connected to something beyond ourselves.

- We feel large, with unlimited possibilities.

- Ego is not present; the Divine is.

- We honor our guidance and intuition.

Understanding contracted and expansive energetic states is important because identifying the states we are currently in will shed light on what playlists we need to use to take us to a different emotional state. If we can identify that we are feeling contracted, our next step will be to pick a more *expansive* emotional state to move into.

Define Your Present Emotional State

Using the Heart Song Breathing Process, take a breath, bringing it up through the bottom of your feet to your heart and releasing the breath through the heart with a sigh.

Now, take a second breath through the top of your head to your heart, and release it through your heart with a sigh.

Finally, take a third breath in through the heart and again out through the heart with a final sigh.

As you breathe through your heart, does your energy feel like it fits the descriptions given above of being expansive or contracted?

If it felt contracted, are you able to pinpoint an emotion that might be contributing to this feeling? For example:

Right now I am in a contracted state of being.
I am feeling sad.

If your energy felt expansive, are you able to pinpoint the emotion that contributes to this feeling? For example:

Right now I am in an expansive state of being.
I am feeling joyous.

Write down your answers. Look at the words you filled in. Let them bring you an awareness of your present state. This is part of meeting yourself where you are at and defining your emotional state in this moment. In order for us to know where we want to go, we have to know where we are. This helps us in dealing with negative emotions instead of pushing them down into our physical body. It also helps us in recognizing the positive emotion behind our expansive states so that we can amplify them even more.

Recognize Your Target Emotional State

Now that you are aware of your present emotional state, let's talk about what's on the other side of the bridge—your target or future emotional state.

Again, use the Heart Song Breathing Process to create a blank palette to work from. Do several repetitions of the three-breath process.

Now, look at your starting phrase and identify the emotion you would like to shift to. For example:

Present state: *Right now I am in a contracted state of being. I am feeling sad.*

Future state: *The emotion I would like to shift to is being happy.*

Or if you were in an expansive state:

Present state*: Right now I am in an expansive state of being. I am feeling joyous.*

Future state: *The emotion I would like to shift to is ecstasy.*

Write your future states down on the opposite side of your paper. Now look at your entries from both sides (present and future). What playlist can you create right now that will take you from one side to the other? Maybe creating a gratitude playlist will shift your sadness to a happier state. Maybe creating an inspirational playlist will amplify your joyous state to an ecstatic one. The choice is yours!

Playlist Construction and Vibrational Metamorphosis

With where you are and where you want to go both defined, the next step is to create the bridge you'll use to move from one state to the next.

Find a quiet place where you won't be interrupted, and give yourself a chance to create your first playlist. Make it a listening experience not just for the ears, but also for the heart and mind. I suggest starting off with music you already have and then investigating new music and uncovering new sound territories. Creating your first playlist can be a life-changing experience. Put your full energy into it. Don't just pick songs—let them pick you. Make it a fun and sacred process. No one will have the exact same playlists as you because no one is exactly the same vibration as you. Your vibration is based on your cumulative experiences.

Incorporate the playlist protocols of volume, tempo, key, genre, rhythm, melody, frequency, and lyrics. Think about the previous discussions of these protocols, and zero in on the ones you feel most drawn to for this particular playlist. Maybe this list will be an experiment in tempo, to move you from a slowed, contracted state to upbeat happiness. Or perhaps the lyrics of certain songs resonate with you today. Mix and match your playlist and explore all the playlist protocols as you feel drawn to do so. Your playlist can be as many or as few songs as you like; usually my playlists have anywhere from three to ten songs.

When you have selected the songs that you want for your first playlist, arrange them in an order that will take you on a powerful journey. Remember the protocols you decided to work with, and put the songs in place to create a path to move you from one state to another. If you decided to work with tempo, maybe you will arrange the slower songs first to gradually build up to the faster songs toward the end of the list, in order to leave you with a peppy, hyped sensation by the end.

You are the orchestrator of your playlists, and there are no wrong answers, so select and arrange the songs as you feel will best serve your intentions. If you are unsure of where to start, use a sample playlist in the back of the book as an example.

Putting Your Playlist into Action

Once you have the playlist you would like to use to create an emotional shift, you'll next need to allow yourself to have the experience. Find an environment that is conducive to listening to the playlist. If your music is geared toward relaxation or inner peace, find a quiet place, light a candle, and make it a sacred experience. If your music is going to ignite, inspire, or create movement, find a space that will allow you to dance or move. Rearrange the furniture, crank the music, and have fun! You might feel your energy shift in one song or you might want to listen to the whole playlist—remember, you are the DJ of your life. Own it!

Shifting Your Emotions and Consciousness

Your playlist is the catalyst to shift your being. Sometimes the shift is subtler, other times it is obvious. If you are able to shift your energy even a little bit that is an amazing start. All of us move through different moods and emotions on a daily basis. It is how long we stay in these moods and emotions that determine a pattern. As emotions move into patterns we can fall into energetic ruts. These ruts create the foundation for building limited belief systems that can move us into challenging times or even life crises. And, as we discussed, these ruts can even begin to affect our physical body.

For example, if as a child I do not feel like my parents trust me, I can begin to have doubts and limited belief systems about moving forward into new areas. In other words, I form challenges in trusting myself. As I get older, when I feel like others do not trust me in my life, it triggers the same energy. This energy can be internalized and can lead to depression and higher levels of stress, both of which may eventually cause chronic health issues.

The amazing thing about using your music playlists on a daily basis is that it can shift those contracted states before they move into patterns. In addition to changing our emotional state, elevating our emotions creates a positive shared field, as we discussed in chapter 2, meaning that as we shift our emotions through our musical playlists, we are sharing this change with everyone in our lives from our heart outward! In other words, when we use music to shift our emotions individually and it enables us to share our gifts, it not only affects our own life, it also affects the lives of everyone around us.

By identifying where you are emotionally and where you want to move next, you can create the *exact* playlist that can take you there. Embrace your power of being the DJ of your life and allow the music that resonates inside of you to uncover the expansive energies that will radiate out from this shared field to imbue your life and the lives of those around you with positive, heartfelt emotions of peace, clarity, and joy!

Sound Tools for Transformation

Here are some powerful suggestions for implementing some of this chapter's concepts to create transformation in your life right now.

- Think of each song that moves you as a precious gift, not just a song in a playlist.

- Use your playlists as a road map to take you toward the energy you need in each situation.

- Become more familiar with the music on the playlists that you have created. Commit to using them when you are feeling out of balance, or when you want to expand and improve on the positive mood you are in.

- Constantly look for new music that will further enhance your playlists, and have fun in the adventure!

Suggested Music

Hopefully you have created your own music playlist(s) in this chapter. Now is the time to embrace your inner DJ and program some music that is perfect in this moment. If you have not yet created your playlist(s), you can refer to the sample playlists provided at the end of the book.

7

Balancing Your Energy Centers

I don't care much about music. What I like is sounds.

—Dizzy Gillespie

IN THE LAST FEW CHAPTERS we covered a great deal of information on how to use music as a tool for healing and personal transformation. In the next three chapters we will explore how to use aspects of sound and vibration to create more balance and harmony in a variety of transformative and healing ways. Just as we used our inner music in the beginning chapters and songs in the last chapter to create personal transformation and improved health, specific sound and vibrational tools can also achieve the same results.

I am passionate about exploring how sound can be used to create transformation in our energetic centers. The energy centers are part of a system that interprets the emotional aspects of our relationships and situations on a daily and momentary basis and communicates this to our four bodies. These centers have also been described as wheels of energy, or chakras, a concept that goes back thousands of years. I think of them as energetic plexes, or fields of information where different aspects of consciousness are held outside our physical body. These subtle energetic plexuses interact with the flow of energy in our physical body.

Seven Energetic Centers

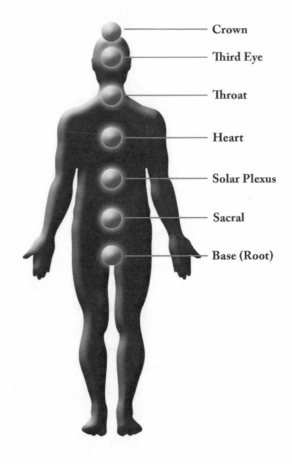

Crown

Third Eye

Throat

Heart

Solar Plexus

Sacral

Base (Root)

Just as our heart emits an energetic field, so do the different energy centers. Similar to our digestive system that manages how food is digested and how we are nourished, the energetic centers manage the energy of situations, events, relationships, and how daily challenges are emotionally digested and create growth that may nourish our souls.

Envision a beautiful handmade guitar made from the finest wood and with breathtaking craftsmanship. Imagine yourself listening to this magnificent guitar. If one of the strings is even slightly out of tune, the instrument is not playing at optimal levels. That one string affects the overall sound or vibration of the whole instrument. Our body is very similar. Our energy centers are like the strings of the guitar. Each center vibrates at a different frequency, and when each is attuned, it aligns with the others perfectly to create the flow of energy that assists our bodies in performing optimally. If one center is out of tune or alignment, like the guitar, the whole instrument does not perform optimally and energy blockages may occur. These blockages can create disharmony, and over a period of time they can manifest as disease in any or all of our four bodies. Just like a guitar, there are ways we can attune our energetic centers utilizing sound and vibrational tools.

When I first started learning about the energy centers many years ago, what excited me was the potential of being able to tune our instrument (our four bodies) through tuning our energy centers. I remember buying my first set of tuning forks and learning how to tune the energy centers. I was amazed that I could feel energy flow in different parts of my body as I tuned the different centers. Years later after doing many, many attunements and seeing their beneficial effects, I am indeed convinced that we can tune ourselves to create optimal energetic flow.

Specific sounds, tones, and even words assist in re-tuning our energies and stored emotions that no longer serve us. This creates space for their higher purpose: to balance and align to create optimal energetic flow. The optimal energetic flow of these centers can bring our four bodies into harmony to create improved health and quality of life.

I look at the energetic centers in a very practical way. Ultimately, we have only so much energy that we can spend. We are all here to share a gift. Whatever it is, if our centers move out of balance from constant drama and upset, we don't have any energy left to spend on our purpose: to share our gifts. Working with and understanding how the energy centers function helps us manage our energy more effectively.

Energy Center/Chakra	Open Emotions	Emotional Blocks
Base/Root (base of the spine)	grounded, supported, nurtured, taken care of	unsupported, in survival mode, or just getting by; feelings of insecurity, depression, frustration, rage; addictions may be present
Sacral (lower abdomen)	joy, passion, and gratitude for our relationships	difficulty digesting daily challenges; a sense of putting up with something or stomaching situations; difficulty expressing emotions; sexual stagnation
Solar Plexus (upper abdomen)	purpose and power; express confidence to others	fear, doubt, lack of confidence, and indecisiveness
Heart	able to give and receive love in perfect balance	bitterness or resentment toward past events; an imbalance of how we give and receive love
Throat	able to communicate and speak our truth effectively	feeling of not being heard, acknowledged, or appreciated by others; Problems not expressing ourselves or overexpressing ourselves
Third Eye (middle of the forehead)	intuition, creativity, and imagination	becoming a prisoner of our thoughts; mind chatter; overanalyzing situations
Crown (top of the head)	a deep spiritual connection to something beyond ourselves	disconnection and confusion; a strong desire to control situations

We have seven basic energetic centers: the base (root), sacral, solar plexus, heart, throat, third eye, and crown. When a center is not balanced, it tends to be blocked or misaligned. When it is balanced, it is open and aligned. As I describe each center, see which descriptions feel like they pertain to certain situations in your life. This will show you which centers may be open or blocked. The energetic centers also have specific attributes that are listed, including a related gland that is its physical counterpart, a color, and a musical note that it resonates with. As the energetic centers go up through our physical body, the musical notes of each center also ascend.

Physical Blocks	Color	Glands	Musical Note
lower back pain, colon issues	red	adrenals	C
stagnant sexually, hip issues	orange	Genitals (testes, ovaries)	D
ulcers, eating disorders, digestive problems	yellow	pancreas	E
heart issues, allergies	green	thymus gland	F
thyroid, throat, and mouth issues	blue	thyroid	G
headaches, eye strain, hormone imbalances	indigo blue	pituitary	A
problems sleeping, light and sound sensitivity	violet	pineal	B

How Energy Centers Can Become Blocked

After having an argument with a friend, I decided to try to patch things up by calling him to see if we could work through the situation. He said he was happy I'd called and began to voice his feelings. Seeing the potential for the situation to be healed, I wanted to be truly present, so I took on the role of the listener. For nearly an hour he detailed my role, my fault in the situation, and my responsibility for making him feel a certain way. He put the blame on me for the pain the situation had caused, and I remained respectfully silent to let him voice his feelings.

After he finished, he stated how much better he felt. Then, before I had a chance to express my side of the situation, he said, "Oh my God, I did not realize it was midnight! I have a big meeting in the morning—can we finish this tomorrow night?" I did not want to escalate the situation when it seemed to be reaching a resolution so I agreed. When I hung up the phone, my throat felt scratchy and I felt like I had a lump in my throat. I realized that not voicing my emotions had caused a blockage in my throat center.

The highest intention of the throat center is to be heard, acknowledged, and appreciated for your words. Although I held the space for the other person to accomplish that, I allowed him to do so at the expense of not speaking my truth. The result was I could feel the emotion literally and physically stuck in my throat.

This happens to us every day. Centers become blocked or fall out of alignment due to stress, trauma, drama, and a host of other situations that can leave us feeling stuck and out of sorts. Thankfully, the energy centers respond to music, sound, and vibration just as readily as our hearts and brains do, so in music we are provided with an easy solution to release the energies that block our centers every day.

My Sound Solution

Although I knew that I would be speaking to my friend the next day, I could not wait to release the energy and emotion that was connected to the situation. It was already manifesting in my physical body. I could feel the phone conversation had really triggered something in me. It felt like getting an electrical shock from touching a battery that is holding a charge. The energy is contained inside the battery and is not released until it is touched by an external source. The argument was the external source.

I attempted to release the energy by journaling about the situation. I hoped that by exploring the emotions of the situation I would also find the charge behind it. I asked myself this powerful question: If this person were here right now and listening compassionately to every word I was saying, what would I want to communicate to him? I began to write nonstop. I could feel my feelings and emotions begin to move as I looked at the words on the page, but there was something missing. My heart was intuitively telling me that I needed to hear the *sound* of the written words vibrating through my throat center. So I stood in front of the mirror with my journal and began to read the words aloud. I could feel the emotions beginning to move out of my throat as the sound of the words vibrated. I could hear the dissonance in the cracks of my voice disappearing. The next thing that happened really surprised me. I began to cry.

In my mind I saw a picture of me sharing my truth with my father when I was about eight years old. My father had fallen asleep at a play and missed an important announcement, but he later denied sleeping and argued with me over the information he had not heard. Looking back as an adult, the situation does not feel as devastating as it did then, but as a child it really hurt me that my dad did not trust my word. I now remember distinctly how I was not heard in the situation and how it felt when he did not believe me. I had been holding this energy for many years, and it had been triggered by not feeling heard during my phone conversation with my friend.

Identifying the source of our triggered emotions is essential, because whenever we bring awareness to these situations we can consciously transform these limiting belief systems into something healing. Because I became aware of the root cause of this blockage, the emotional charge had lessened in each situation where I was challenged to speak my truth.

As I heard, acknowledged, and appreciated my own voice (the highest intention of the throat center), it realigned into a more balanced state. I felt as if the message had been delivered to my friend even without speaking to him. The next day, there was very little charge left when I had the opportunity to speak with him about my feelings. What started out as dissonance was transmuted into harmony and our argument became the vehicle for a stronger friendship.

In my work assisting individuals in clearing their centers, I see even more pronounced blockages that cause physical symptoms of discomfort and illness. In one session, I had a client who was experiencing severe hives. As the session unfolded, she began to tell me about the stress her job was creating. Within that conversation she described the situation at work as "toxic." She also informed me she had been "putting up with it" and was looking for a new job. I asked her if it would be accurate to describe her situation as something she was "stomaching" or "having a hard time digesting." This question opened the floodgates and she began to cry. In addition to the hives, she had been experiencing stomach issues, indigestion, and severe diarrhea. The emotional toxicity she was experiencing at work was having an effect on her physical body and was surfacing through her skin and within her stomach. We created an energetic game plan for coping while she looked for a new job. The next time I saw her, she informed me she had found a new job and her hives had disappeared.

Transformation can occur in an instant when we find a core issue that is blocking an energetic center and release it. Sometimes we have to unveil the subconscious emotions that are being held. Each center plays a role in our lives and has specific emotional energy that relates to it.

In every challenge we encounter, we have an opportunity to embrace the gift of each center and move the emotion so it does not become blocked. When this occurs, we bring harmony to the energetic center. When the emotion is withheld and not expressed, that specific center can become energetically blocked. Eventually, this lack of energetic flow can affect our physical body and move into a place of dissonance. Your body is indeed your personal instrument, and emotions can be the catalyst that can keep your health in tune or can become the badly sung note that creates stress and disharmony in the body.

The Three-Step Process for Optimal Energy Flow

Once we find the emotional charge of a situation, or the root cause of the blockage, we can identify the energetic centers that are blocked using the sound of the breath and toning. We can work with releasing the energy held in those centers through sounding trigger words or phrases that hold the charge of the situation. The last part of the session is attuning the energy centers with tuning forks and clearing the energetic field. If you don't have tuning forks, there are other ways to tune the centers that are discussed at the end of this chapter. In addition, during my private sessions, I play designer music that I have created that takes my clients to a deep state of relaxation which helps to re-entrain them with their heart and gives their physical, mental, emotional, and spiritual bodies a chance to rejuvenate and integrate their session. I have found that this three-step process of Identifying, Releasing, and Attuning is an amazing way to create optimal energetic flow in our centers.

Identify Energetic Blocks

The first step in working with the energetic centers is to find out if the centers are in optimal flow. Of course, we can have a person who does energy or healing work balance our centers; but if we don't know what took them out of balance in the first place, the same situations may block them again. Luckily, there are a couple quick and easy ways to use sound to determine if one or more of your centers is currently blocked.

Using the Breath

Start off by placing your hand on the corresponding location of the energetic center you wish to investigate. (Refer to the chart on pages 74–75 if you need a refresher.)

Physically touching the center creates a focus for where to send the breath. Bring a deep breath in through the center and release a big sigh out through the center. Do this several times. Bringing the sound of your life-force (your breath coming in and sigh going out) through each center can begin to open and move energy. Very often, when energy begins to move we can determine if it feels open and expansive or closed and contracted, as discussed in the last chapter.

As you breathe through the area, notice if the energy is moving through it, or if it feels stuck. Does the area feel contracted or expansive? Does the energy feel heavy or light? Don't judge yourself; simply begin to identify what centers feel expansive and which feel contracted.

Go through all seven centers and take notes on how each one feels. Reflect on your notes after you finish to see where you feel the most contracted and the most expansive.

Using Toning

The breath is a transformational tool to bring a gentle awareness to which energetic centers are open and expansive and which are contracted or closed. The next step is combining the breath with toning through the different centers. Although there are many variations, the following are the tones I have been utilizing with benefit:

Center	Sound
Base	U pronounced "you"
Sacral	O pronounced "oh"
Solar Plexus	A pronounced "aaay"
Heart	AH pronounced "ahhhh"
Throat	I pronounced "eye"
Third Eye	E pronounced "eee"
Crown	Eh pronounced "ehhh"

Using the base center as an example, gently place your hand on this center. Bring the biggest breath you can into the base of your spine and release the lowest, deepest and longest pitch of U through the center as you release the breath. Try this several times, utilizing your breath to push the sound out. The idea is to find the exact sound that feels like it makes that area vibrate.

Notice if you are able to feel the sound move through the center effortlessly or if it feels stuck. Does it feel closed and contracted or open and expansive?

As you did with the breath exercise on page 65, go through each center, placing your hands on each one as you practice your tones. As you move through the different tones for each center, the note should get higher. It does not have to be pretty. (My dog Woody often leaves the room when I am toning through the centers.)

After you go through all of the centers take some notes on which ones you had challenges with. What centers felt contracted or blocked in both exercises? These are the centers you will focus on.

When I had major dental procedures done and prescription drugs were only marginally helping the pain, I decided to incorporate some sound tools to assist in diminishing the pain and anxiety associated with the dental work. Toning into tight areas in our body can loosen the stressors we are holding and bring them to the surface to be released.

In the case of my dental work, I began to tone different sounds into the area in my mouth that was experiencing pain, searching for the resonant tone that would release it. Through trial and error I found the tone and then the pain diminished considerably. This process can also be utilized for other areas and centers of the body.

The mouth is under the domain of the energetic center of the throat, which is about speaking one's truth and knowing that the words are heard, acknowledged, and appreciated. As we actively engage our mouth and throat area through vocally toning, we are taking a powerful role in our own healing process. We are able to utilize our voice as a carrier of our emotions to break up stagnant energy in our physical body. Our voice is being heard, acknowledged, and appreciated by ourselves, which sets the space for others to do the same.

Release Negative Energy

In order to bring new, higher vibrational energy or elevated emotions into the centers, and attune them to their highest potential, it is important to release negative emotions that we are holding on to. This could be energy that you are holding consciously from a situation that happened yesterday or an event that you are holding in your subconscious from years ago. It's like cleaning out your closet. If you want to buy a new wardrobe, you have to make room for it. If you are still holding on to that cheerleading uniform from high school or a bowling ball in the back of your closet, they are taking up space. Just like those items, it's time to clear out old energy.

I like to use trigger words and phrases for each of the centers that assist in releasing negative stored emotional energy. If you are holding negative energy or emotions in the centers, you will feel a resonance, a charge, or a magnification of the energy being held in the area when you read the trigger words. Trigger words and phrases represent the possible energy being held in each center and help to bring awareness of what it might be related to.

Center	Trigger Words and Phrases
Base	survival/fight-or-flight mode; addiction; not having enough or not feeling nurtured or supported; money issues
Sacral	stomaching or putting up with a situation; having a hard time digesting something or someone
Solar Plexus	lack of trust, doubt, second-guessing, fear
Heart	holding resentment, bitterness
Throat	feeling unheard, unappreciated, or unable to speak one's truth
Third Eye	repetitive mind chatter, stuck in a story, reliving issues in the past
Crown	deadlines and commitments, time constraints; spiritual disconnection

As you read the trigger words for each center, which ones relate to situations that are going on in your life? Do they coincide with the centers that felt blocked during the breathing and toning exercises?

Close your eyes for a moment and take some slow breaths from the bottom of your feet all the way up to your head and then let the breath move back to your feet before you release it. This creates more energetic flow and helps to release any stagnant energy you are holding. Do this several times until you begin to feel lighter.

Now that you have the energy moving, you will release the energies from specific, contracted centers. In each center, release the energy of the trigger words by breathing into the center and then releasing a sound. Each sound should be connected to the emotion being held. If you feel angry, let the sound symbolize that anger, such as a shout or a yell; if you feel sad, cry.

Once you have gone through the center sounding the emotion, it's time to do the final sweep. Review the trigger words for the center you are working with, but this time add "I release" in front of them (refer to the chart on page 83). For example, in the base center, say: "I release addiction, not having enough, or not feeling nurtured or supported." Take a big breath in and make a sound to release the emotion held in the energy center. Continue to do this with each energetic center. When you are done, gently breathe through each center one more time, allowing yourself to feel lighter, more open, and expansive.

Attune

Now that you have identified what centers were blocked and have released some of the negative emotions that were being held there, let's attune the centers to their optimal vibration. The energetic centers can be tuned in many ways, including crystal bowls, toning and chanting, crystals, stones, color, light, essential oils, healing touch, tuning forks, and with intention, songs, and words. While we don't have the space to cover all these healing modalities here, we will cover using tuning forks, intention, and songs.

Tuning Forks

Working with tuning forks is based on the principle that each of the energetic centers resonates with a unique vibration or frequency.

I think of the energetic centers as a spiritual antenna. When the antenna is completely straight, we get the best reception and we can truly "tune in." When a center is out of alignment, it's as if the antenna is bent and our reception is not optimal. Tuning forks can assist us in bringing the centers back into alignment. As we strike each fork, the vibrational frequency of the fork is sounded.

We then place the tuning fork over the optimal position of each center. The tone or note of the tuning fork resonates with the same frequency of the energetic center (see the musical notes listed in the energetic center descriptions on pages 74–75) and, almost like a magnet, the fork moves the center back into alignment to create optimal flow. This is done with each of the seven centers until they are all in alignment.

Of course, if we don't work on the issues that create the blocks, the centers will move back out of alignment. That is why we work on identifying the blocks and releasing them before we attune them.

Tuning Through Intention

By understanding the highest intention of each center we can gauge what situations, challenges, people, places, and things pull us away from that intention and how we can avoid giving our energy away. Each intention starts off with the words *I Am*. This is one of the names of God in Hebrew. When we bring these words into the intention of each of the centers, we bring in the power of connecting our hearts with the heart of the creator. Our intention is connected to the highest potential to create in this way. As you connect with each center, bring a focus to that area again by placing your hand on each center. Give yourself a breath in and speak the following intentions out loud after releasing your breath. Continue to breathe in and out of the energetic center, allowing the energy to integrate and balance, then move to the next center.

Center	Intention
Base	I am safe, supported, and nurtured in the world. I am grounded and focused as I walk the path of my soul's purpose.
Sacral	I am a sensual being and joyous in my relations. I am able to digest situations and events in my life without drama.
Solar Plexus	I am confident and powerfully centered in my purpose.
Heart	I am a vehicle of giving and receiving love in perfect balance.
Throat	I am a speaker of truth and I am heard, acknowledged, and appreciated.
Third Eye	I am an intuitive vessel. I honor the guidance and wisdom I receive.
Crown	I am connected to the source of all that is. I am aligned with the fullest potential of my spiritual essence.

Tuning Through Song

Utilizing songs that carry the optimal intention for each energy center is another fun way to balance and harmonize each center. You can listen to the songs anywhere and also make a transformative shift in a short amount of time. Below are some musical suggestions for each center and a rationale for why I picked each song. As you listen, I suggest placing your hand on each of the center's locations and gently breathing in and out of them as you listen.

Center	Song Choice
Base	"Drum Dance" by Barry Goldstein—This song incorporates powerful drums with beautiful low frequencies that will help you feel more grounded and supported.
Sacral	"Swadhisthana" by Vive—The gentle chanting of mantras combined with the soulful singing and sensual movement of percussion set the perfect tone for cleansing and balancing this center.
Solar Plexus	"Conquest of Paradise" by Vangelis—For moving into a state where you are owning your power and stepping into your purpose. The powerful epic drums and pulsating orchestral strings are a call to embrace your magnificence! If you are looking for a sonic jumpstart to spark your day in less than five minutes, this is a great piece.
Heart	"Shores of Avalon" by Tina Malia—This song invites you to a place where fear is gone. The honesty of Tina Malia's voice with the heart-opening cellos will gently pry away your inner fears, give you comfort, and allow you to tune in to a fuller knowing of your beautiful heart.
Throat	"Om Namo Narayanaya" by Deva Premal—If you are looking for a perfect way to open and balance your throat center, there is nothing like a sing-a-long chant. Connect with the purity of her voice to find the purity and power of your own. Chant with her for five minutes in your day and know that you are heard, acknowledged, and appreciated!
Third Eye	"Third Eye Chakra Light Vision" by Dean Evenson—By surrendering the thoughts of situations beyond your control, and clearing energy in your mind, you can tap into the intuitive gifts that are engaged in the third eye center. This song sets the space for surrender. The beautiful strokes of the guitar and ethereal flute colorings paint the perfect musical landscape to erase mind chatter and tap into your powerful, intuitive self.
Crown	"The Light" by Michael Chorvat—If you want a slightly different approach, use this rock song to clear this center. This song will assist in clearing stagnant energy that connects the physical body to the light, the source of all creation!

The Benefits of Optimal Flow in Our Energy Centers

I invite you to try the different ways to create balance in the energetic centers that we've covered. There are many paths on the road to optimal energetic flow. The more we work with our energetic centers, the more effectively we are able to manage our life situations and challenges on a daily basis. Here are a few of the benefits of this practice:

- We become more grounded and focused.

- Our relationships are more harmonious.

- We experience more joy.

- We experience less stress and anxiety.

- We give and receive in a more balanced way.

- We communicate better.

- We follow our intuition.

- We spend less energy reacting or overreacting in situations and move to a state of responsibility where we choose our response (our ability to respond).

A well-known law of nature, the ripple effect, comes into play when we begin to work with our energetic centers. The ripple effect says that when you drop a stone in a calm, serene pond, it ripples outward from its center. When our energy centers are aligned in their highest functions and intentions, they also ripple outwardly from their center to affect our relationships, our community, and beyond in positive ways. This is why it is important to incorporate balancing your energy centers into your daily musical program!

Sound Tools for Transformation

Here are some powerful suggestions for implementing some of this chapter's concepts to create transformation in your life right now.

- Move through the process of attuning your centers during your week. Light some candles and balance your centers through one of the tuning processes described in this chapter. Constantly upgrade your awareness of what centers feel open, in balance, and expansive and what centers feel closed, out of balance, or contracted.

- As your week unfolds, see what issues feel like they are taking you out of balance. Can you identify what center the issue relates to? If the same person or situation is taking you out of balance, create a boundary of how much energy you are willing to spend on it before you become drained.

- Use the energy center vowels and tones provided in the chapter to open the centers and create more optimal flow.

Suggested Music

Choose (and use!) one of the energy center songs in this chapter when you are feeling a block in that center. This is a quick and fun way to create awareness, move stagnant energy, and transform to a more expansive state in each center.

8

Expansion and Connection Through Chanting, Sound, and Vibration

He who sings scares away his woes.

—Cervantes

In 2006, my dad was diagnosed with bladder cancer. Over the course of that next year, I saw his physical body diminish. Although his body was transitioning, there was healing that was occurring in our family structure, and I believe my dad was holding on to accommodate that.

The day before he passed, I found myself alone in my father's hospital room. This was the first time I had been alone with him in over a year. It was also the first time my mother had been away from him, and although she regretted not being there, I know my being alone with him was for a purpose. As I stood by his bedside, he was mostly unconscious. His eyes were rolling in his head but he was still fighting to stay. I'm not sure if he was aware that I was in the room. Then something very strange happened. I heard an inner voice guiding me to sing to him. I tried to ignore it, but I heard it again. In my head I answered, *What do you want me to sing?* I heard back, *Just sing.*

I felt ridiculous; I didn't know what to sing. So, I closed my eyes and went into my heart. In a moment I found myself very close to him at his headboard with my hand on top of his head. I felt myself toning into the top of his head and I began to feel warmth emanate. As I continued to sing different tones I could feel his energy releasing weight and getting lighter from the top of his head. Expanding. When I opened my eyes my dad was looking directly at me. He was conscious and aware. I was amazed. I asked if he could hear me, and although he could not really speak he nodded his head. In that moment, I was able to truly tell my dad what he meant to me. He acknowledged me and nodded as I spoke. I told him not to be afraid and I thanked him for all he had given me. It was the most amazing conversation we had ever had, so much of it without words.

That night my dad left his physical body. After holding on for a long time he was finally able to let go. I believe that chanting and toning assisted in opening his top energetic center so his soul could leave his physical body with grace and ease. The crown center is a bridge between the physical and ethereal bodies. A primary function of chanting is to amplify our spiritual connection and deepen our relationship with God. This was the beginning of my journey in truly understanding the power of chanting.

Chanting

The word *chant* comes from the French word *chanter,* which means to sing. Chants may range from a simple melody involving a few notes to more complex melodies using many notes.

In essence, the common chord that weaves through chanting in many cultures and religions is that chant is a way to expand our spiritual connection. It enables us to convey our emotions in another form than traditional speech. It is a way for us to have an experience beyond our intellectual thought process. In fact, chanting is the perfect practice to move out of negative, repetitive thought patterns and mind chatter. It can be done individually or in a group setting and is considered a strong pathway to spiritual development.

Chanting is also an excellent tool to incorporate into your daily musical program to calm the busy mind. Most of us have experienced repetitive internal dialogue at different times in our lives. Replaying a future event over and over in our minds in an effort to uncover the many possible outcomes, or reliving a situation that has already occurred, can cause a great deal of stress. Listening to and participating in music that features repetitive chanting occupies and focuses our attention on musical and tonal phrases and can take us out of destructive, repetitive internal dialogue. As our focus shifts, the story and stress can be freed and we can move back into a more harmonious state. Chanting takes us out of our normal time continuum and allows us to tame our ego. As this occurs, we move to a deeper state of relaxation.

Seed Syllables

A powerful way to become acquainted with the power of chanting is through the chanting of *om.* The sound and syllable of the word *om,* or *aum,* is said to contain every sound in the universe and weaves through many languages. That is why it is called a seed syllable. When we chant the word *om,* we expand our energetic field and open our connection to the Divine. Although it sounds like a one-syllable word, *om* is broken down into four syllables, each with a different meaning.

Aah

The *aah* sound represents the creation aspects of the universe.

Within the sound of *aah* we connect with ourselves on a physical level. The sound resonates in the lower abdomen and throat.

Oooh

The *U* sound (pronounced *oooh*) expands our focus and connects us to a higher power, which helps us open up to clarity and expand our essence of light.

Mmmm

This sound unites us to the essence of oneness. It vibrates at the crown of our head and bridges our physical and ethereal bodies and opens us up to a deeper spiritual connection. As we open up to this connection, we allow ourselves to pause and feel all that is.

(Silence)

The fourth sound is silence. This is where we integrate the experience beyond words and feel it in our physical and energetic bodies. It's the space between the sounds. Breathe that in. Allow yourself to hear and experience the silence.

I invite you to experiment with each of the syllables; chant them separately and together, allow them to move through your body, mind, and spirit. Practice in five-minute intervals. Then work your way up to chanting *om* for twenty minutes during your week as part of your musical practice. You will be amazed by the transformational results!

Utilizing *om* is a great starting point on the journey to using chanting as a healing tool, and it is always powerful. Because it contains every sound in the universe, we never outgrow it, no matter where we are on our path. Many cultures and spiritual practices also chant additional mantras, which can be just as helpful and can assist many different areas of our health.

Mantras

A mantra is words or sounds repeated to aid concentration in meditation. The origins of the mantra date back over three thousand years and now are used in many religious and spiritual practices. Utilizing repetitive mantras can be a great aid in moving to a relaxed state, and it is also a wonderful way to use the sound of your words to move through anxiety and release mind chatter.

While the chanting of mantras has been used religiously for thousands of years, I believe we can also create our own mantras, even if we are not religious. We can utilize the same principles but customize them to transform negative emotions, anxiety, and mental and physical stress.

Creating a Daily Mantra Exercise

Think of something that is going on in your life right now and is bringing anxiety or stress or is draining the positive energy out of your day. Keep this situation in mind as you create a daily mantra to help you manage these circumstances.

Think about the energy of the situation and try to represent the negative aspects or feelings associated with a few words. For example, if you are in a situation where you're unsure of yourself, the negative aspects might be: doubt, fear, and uncertainty. Write down the negative words that represent the situation.

Now that you are looking at these words, you can see how heavy they feel. They carry a vibration that might be draining your energy.

Think of three words that would act as a remedy for you and would bridge your current state to a more positive state. For example, three words that would be a remedy to doubt, fear, and uncertainty are trust, love, and clarity. Write down these words as well.

When you look at the three positive words on your paper you will see they feel much lighter. Read them and feel them until they are memorized.

Begin to chant the positive words. Let the sound flow from your throat and find your own rhythm with them. As you become more comfortable, play with the volume and intensity of the words and put emotion and feeling into them. If you hear a melody, feel free to sing!

Chant the mantra until you feel lighter and more relaxed.

Congratulations! Now you have another sound tool to plug into your daily musical practice. Create different mantras as they are needed in your day and know that you have the power to shift your day with sound.

The great thing about chanting is that there are no external tools that you have to buy or carry with you. The voice that you have been given is a powerful tool that you can use anytime during your day. Studies have shown that chanting increases blood flow to the brain, provides exercise to the lungs and chest, and improves pulmonary function.[18]

I invite you to incorporate chanting into your daily musical practice. Even five minutes can help you to release stress you are holding in your body before it becomes a more significant physical challenge.

The Sound of Prayer

Although prayer is thought of as being part of a religious practice, prayer is also a way to deepen our spiritual connection and relationship beyond religion in a more intimate and individual way. Prayer is a vibrational tool that is sounding a communication with God. As we hear our inner and outer voice, we are sounding, acknowledging, and processing the situation in a different way. We are having an experience from our soul's center. I have found that in this spiritual communion my whole being releases a sigh. The process of voicing our most personal inner thoughts can shift our emotions and assist us in releasing challenges and any unresolved issues that we are holding. For thousands of years, music and prayer have danced hand in hand. When we sing hymns in church, chant in Hebrew, or say *om* in Sanskrit, they become a catalyst to bring the prayer into action, magnifying the words with music to amplify the experience.

Drumming and Coherence

For those of you who want alternatives to using your voice, drumming is a wonderful option. A great way to resynchronize, move into rhythm, and connect with others is through a drum circle. When we drum, it is symbolic of the heartbeat that exists in all of us; it represents the common thread that weaves us together. In a drum circle, we have the opportunity to participate and experience the different frequencies of the drums and their role in creating coherence. The low floor drum that connects us to Mother Earth carries a simple but powerful heartbeat. The high frequency of the small shakers connects us to the energy of Father Sky and keeps a constant moving pace. The mid frequencies of the hand drums fill in, syncopate, and vary the rhythm.

Feeling our internal drum (our heart) entrain with the drums we are playing is a very beautiful and powerful feeling. Although the drums and players vary, there is an underlying order that is occurring. This order assists in creating more coherence in our physical body as well.

As we participate in the circle and switch drums, we have the ability to understand that each drum has a different role. As one drum changes, it changes the whole rhythm, just as each one of us changing affects the transformation of the whole planet. Understanding the relationship of the drum and the drummer allows us to understand the dance of life.

Our roles in the dance of life, just as in the drum circle, are constantly changing and transforming. Our vibration changes based on situations and events that occur in our lives, and very often we need to resynchronize and find the rhythm within a situation. Bringing order where disorder exists creates coherence in our lives as well as our bodies. Just as we have to find the rhythm to drum to a song we are hearing for the first time, new challenges require us to shift and let go of rigidity. As we learn to bend and flow when it is required, transformation awaits with each new step learned.

Sound Tools For Transformation

Here are some practical ways to incorporate this chapter's teachings into your daily program:

- Take a few moments to incorporate the *om* chant in your day when your energy feels contracted. As you hear the sound emanate from your voice, surrender control of a situation and allow the sound to cleanse your mind chatter.

- Create your own mantras to chant when you are experiencing stress, pain, or tightness. Draw from the positive words you wrote down, and let the mantra move through your voice, creating a shift within your being. Make this a part of your healing process!

- Consider buying some type of percussive instrument to channel your energy. Tambourines, shakers, and hand percussion are reasonably priced and a great way to find your rhythm. Practice keeping rhythm with one of your favorite songs or see if there is a drumming circle in your area.

Suggested Music

- "Om Mantra" by Deva Premal and Miten—The exotic instrumentation of this piece invites you into a very pure, sacred space. The clear, lush voice of Deva Premal invites you to chant *om* and connect with the Divine.

- "Om Shalom Home" by Barry Goldstein—This beautiful chant was created based on the seed syllables discussed in this chapter. As we chant "Om Shalom Home," we bring the intention of joining cultures together with the universal language of love—music.

9

The Vibration of Words and Intention

Music washes away from the soul the dust of everyday life.

—Berthold Auerbach

THE POWER OF WORDS IS WELL KNOWN. We have all experienced instances when words have comforted us. I remember in a time of emotional crisis, a friend told me in a very soothing and heartfelt way, "Everything is going to be okay." I know it seems simple, but there was so much kindness and authenticity in the sound of her voice that I was deeply moved in knowing that her words resonated with truth.

Words are not always included in this topic of sound and vibration, and yet they can be an amazing sound tool to create change. It is said that in some religions the whole universe was created by the word of God. We can also create our own universe or world with our words. The internal and external words you use on a daily basis tell a story to your body. Just like music, the words you speak can create harmony or dissonance in your four bodies. If you are repeatedly using negative phrases or words to describe a situation and they are coupled with negative emotions such as fear or anger, what is this telling your physical body? What are your words composing and orchestrating in your life?

I have a friend who was diagnosed with cancer and created an amazing shift by changing one word . . . chemo. After realizing that this word was creating anxiety and stress, both of which had the potential of hindering his healing process, he began using the word "treatment" instead. The word created a feeling that was more calming to him and instigated a different conversation with his body and his mind, one that could be more conducive to his healing process. Now imagine how replacing the words "life-threatening" or "chronic" with the term "health challenge" could diminish the energy of the not-so-happy ending you are telling your physical body.

Many times, we are speaking to our body on a subconscious level and don't even realize that we have been composing a not-so-pretty song. We have been creating a state of dissonance and have not realized that we are steering ourselves into disharmony. But we can get back on the right path by using the power and sound of our words coupled with intention.

Our intentions create a vibratory field that is produced from our thoughts, words, and emotions. When the field becomes strong enough, it can attract similar vibrations to manifest the intention.

Music is an excellent example of how intention can create and effect a vibratory field. When I compose music, I create an intention to evoke a certain feeling in the listener. The combination of notes and putting my specific targeted emotions into the music creates a feeling that is felt beyond myself. The people in the room listening also feel it.

Setting an intention consists of *doing* something (an action) and *becoming* the emotion of the action. For example, if you want to see love, be love. I call this combining "to do" and "to be." Another example is, if I want to set the intention of creating joy in the people listening to my music, I choose a chord that has specific notes that sound joyful. The action of playing the chord is the "to do." When I embed my actual feelings and emotions of joy into the chord as I play, this is the "to be." By putting the emotion (to be) into the action (to do), I am sparking the intention into motion by providing it with new information. When you, the listener, hear the chord being played combined with the emotion, you move beyond just hearing the emotion—you feel it.

Words are no different. When we create intention, we are setting a purpose with our words and emotions. When words and emotions align, we create an attraction pattern that can manifest the intention created, just as in the music example given above. Similar to playing the piano, words move beyond the person composing them and affect the listener. Think of the universe as the listener and the eager audience that awaits the beautiful composition of your intention and then responds with a vibratory match. Let me share a powerful story of how intention manifested in my life!

The Les Paul Guitar

I was about fourteen when my parents decided they would fulfill my dream of having an electric guitar. I had been playing and writing songs for about two years, and the family concerts (my sister on piano and me on guitar) were getting more frequent. They gave me a budget of two hundred dollars and I had decided on a Fender Telecaster. We went to the House of Music in New Rochelle and I tried a bunch of guitars. We had almost decided on one when the salesman asked if he could show us one more.

He realized he had a live one on the hook and came back with a hard case with GIBSON printed on it. I can still see the hot pink lush velvet interior lining (a lá the 1970s) stimulating my young eyes, but not as much as the gleaming Gibson Les Paul cherry sunburst guitar. "Oh my God, that's the guitar Jimmy Page and Carlos Santana play!" I said in excitement. I think it was then that my dad realized he was in trouble. He knew those were my favorite players. I could see the emotion in his eyes as he asked to talk to me for a moment. "You know your mother's going to kill me if I get you this guitar," he said, which was pretty funny considering how small my mom was. He continued, "If I buy you this guitar, you have to promise me that you're going to stick with music."

I was fourteen—of course I promised. As soon as I promised, I remember my dad going to the car. He came back with a dusty French horn that was in the trunk and put it on the counter to trade in. He laid down a few credit cards next to the French horn to complete the transaction. I can still feel that heavy case digging into my little hands as I carried my new Gibson Les Paul back to the car.

Years later, I realized that in that moment I made more than a promise; I made a commitment so strong that it seeded a destiny for music to be in my life forever. I created an intention. Over many years, I would look at the name LES PAUL embedded into the guitar, and it became a symbol of my parents' belief in me, imbued with positive and elevated emotion. This repeated event created an energetic field that moved into harmony and alignment beyond my wildest imagination.

No matter how tempted I was to sell that guitar in my early years of financial struggle, I never could or would. The universe responded, and thirty years later I ended up working with the inventor of the electric guitar, Les Paul, on a tribute album for his ninetieth birthday. The song I coproduced, called "69 Freedom Special," won the Grammy for Best Rock Instrumental in 2005. I strongly believe this never would have manifested if it weren't for that guitar. Every time I looked at it, I was reminded of my dad's faith in me, despite his own limited beliefs. This emotional response became a type of soul food that nourished the intention I had planted in the promise to my dad. I became the frequency of that Les Paul guitar, and the rest is history!

How to Set Your Intention

Now it's time for you to tap into the power of your intention. The intention you create can be an activation of your gifts, your purpose, or hidden desires that are held within your heart. When creating an intention, I always ask myself, *If the universe were listening to me in this moment (which it is) and I could manifest and co-create anything with it (which I can), what would that be?* Take a moment to ask yourself that question now and write down the answer. As you read these words, do they create a calling to your heart that cannot be ignored? This is where the most powerful intentions are seeded.

It's important to communicate clearly, especially when setting your intention. If you are using the words "I want," you are telling the universe you are missing something. Fine-tune it with higher vibrational words such as "I choose." If you are using the word "try," it carries a heavy vibration, like you are trying to walk up the mountain or saying there is room for failure. Replace "try" with "creating": I am *creating* the moment of walking up the mountain.

Every word holds a unique vibration. It should be like music to the ears of the universe. Remember, you are the conductor. Take a moment to fine-tune the words that you have written down.

The intention you have written down is your action or your *to-do*. Now, what is the emotion you would like to hold the to-do in? This is the chalice that holds your sacred intention; it could be love, it could be courage, it could be passion. Go into your heart and feel it. Place your hands on your heart; take a breath into your heart and a breath out through your heart. Tap into your music within, and feel and become the emotion of your intention. When you have it, open your eyes and write it down. This is the *to-be* of your intention.

When you combine your to-do with your to-be, your intention is nurtured, nourished, and sparked into action. In addition, visualize the intention has already happened and then let it go. This combination is powerful and can activate an intention—even if it doesn't manifest immediately.

Using Songs to Optimize Intention

To boost your clarity of intention, choose songs that correspond with the emotion you are trying to convey. If you want joy as your *to-be* in your intention, then I suggest listening to joyous songs (or your joy playlist) as you settle in to get clear about your intention.

I'm sure you've listened to a piece of music and felt the song was written for you. The composer's feelings were so authentic that they created a strong emotional resonance that awakened and magnified something within you. I'm also sure you have experienced a song in which the emotions did not match the message. The singer's intention might have been to create a certain state, but the outcome was not received.

Just like the energies we put out as we create our intentions, all of these subtle energies come through in music as well, so make sure you choose a piece of music that really moves you to a clear, coherent emotional state before you set your intention to help you fine-tune and optimize it for your benefit. Continue to utilize this piece of music as part of your daily practice to reconnect you with your intention and to nurture it.

Conscious Entrainment

As we set our intention and create a vibratory field, it is important to take on the role of the conscious observer. Just as a gardener cares for his or her garden to make sure weeds don't take over the fertile terrain, you are the gardener of your own energetic field. When you create this field from your clear and pure intention, your vibration is very high; you are optimistic and your intention is aligned. When you share an intention with someone, you invite his or her energy into this field. Up until this point, your intention was only shared with the universe. Before you invite someone in to share or support your intention, envision yourself sharing your intention with him or her.

The intention you have created is like a beautiful piece of music. Is this person you've selected to share it with singing along and harmonizing with you? Do his or her words sound like someone who cannot carry a tune?

When someone is bringing harmony to your energetic field,

- There is a supportive energy that feels aligned with the words they are speaking.

- If there is critique, it is constructive and the points they make strengthen your intention.

- You feel inspired, ignited, and energetic after speaking with them.

- Your intention and energetic field feels stronger.

- You feel like they are part of your ultimate support team.

When someone is bringing dissonance to your energetic field,

- There is an underlying energy that does not feel supportive, although his or her words may seem to be.

- The success of your intention might be questioned and undermined without constructive criticism.

- You feel energetically drained after speaking with the person.

- The intention you shared does not feel as strong to you; you are less excited about it or are questioning it after your conversation.

- You don't feel like you want to share your intention with this person again.

You are the orchestrator of your field, and you get to decide who is harmonizing and who is creating discordant notes. You do not need to let those who create dissonance into your field. Keep your intention clean and your boundaries firm to support yourself in staying true to what you want to create in your life.

When you are not aware, you can unconsciously entrain with lower vibrational or negative emotions others carry and allow them to punch energetic holes in your field and your intention. Before you know it, your intention has diminished and you're not sure why. If you are not able to bring harmony to the situation, then pull the weed from the garden or withdraw from depending on this person's support. You require the ultimate spiritual team for support, and you are worth it!

As we become more aware of how we spend our energy, we can begin to fine-tune ourselves and our relationships so dissonance is limited. We begin to know ourselves on a deeper level and find harmony with ourselves and others. Utilizing music, sound, and vibration and applying the tools, techniques, and processes is an important step to this awareness. Keep your instrument attuned on a daily basis and ignite the powerful emotions within you to maintain the path of living a musical life.

Sound Tools for Transformation

Here are some powerful suggestions for implementing some of this chapter's concepts to create transformation in your life right now.

- If the universe was listening to every thought and word you were saying (and it is), what intention would you create?

- Find a song that will complement or enhance your intention. You may use the song below, or a song from one of your playlists.

Suggested Music

"Words" by Stephanie Mckenna—A heart-opening and inspirational song about the power our words have to mold our lives and the lives of others. A great way to open space before you set your intention for the day!

10

Ignite Your Creativity with Music

*The function of music is to release us
from the tyranny of conscious thought.*

—Sir Thomas Beecham, English conductor

ALBERT EINSTEIN UNDERSTOOD how music fed the creative process. His wife said that whenever he was stuck on a problem that seemed insurmountable, he would play chords on the piano to clear his mind. When he came back to the problem afterward, he often broke through his mental blocks and was able to tackle the problem from a new, energized state of being. Music helped him to move out of his logical mind into pure creativity, where the greatest breakthroughs became possible.

Creativity allows us to stretch into unchartered territories and expand our consciousness. As we move into the creative process, we tap into our imagination and our intuition. In addition, we are utilizing both our mind's intelligence and our heart's intelligence, yet we are also connecting to the intelligence outside ourselves. When we connect with this universal source that has created everything, we draw from infinite creative possibilities beyond our limited experiences.

Creating Divine Collaborations

Nature is the music of the universe and orchestrates beauty in every moment. Before you start your creative process, I invite you to take a walk in nature. Listening to the sounds of nature is a miraculous experience that allows us to deepen our spiritual connection and experience a feeling that there is something beyond us that has a wild and vivid imagination and an amazing sense of creation. You can call it the Universe, the Divine, Creator, or God—but what is truly important is that by connecting with nature and the amazing array of sounds it provides, we bring in the potential to tap into its infinite possibilities, boundless imagination, and limitless outcomes and channel that source into our own creations.

I begin my creative process by inviting that source to create with me. I used to dream of collaborating with Bono from U2. No offense to Bono, but God blows him out of the water! These divine collaborations have changed my creative process. God is in a constant state of creation, and we can be as well. When we allow ourselves to become the vessel that God flows through, we are no longer in charge and are able to release ourselves to the creativity that pours out of us.

In 2002, I received a song by special delivery: in a dream. At the time, I had been reading Neale Donald Walsch's book *Conversations with God*, and I was affected deeply. It's hard to describe this dream because the experience was really beyond words. I have heard many say "We are all one," but up until this dream I had never truly experienced it.

In the dream, I was shown how we are all connected from the perspective of a blade of grass. Everything that passed me was seen and felt as a miracle in every cell of my body. The scent within the breeze, the blue within the sky, the mist within the rain, *everything*! Even though *I was* the blade of grass, I was *also* the breeze, the scent within the breeze, the mist within the rain, the blue within the sky, and they were me. I was everything and everything was me. Everything had a direct effect on everything else. There was no separation. I was given the gift of seeing things "through the eyes of God." In the dream I heard the words to the chorus as clear as day. The melody came with it and was quite haunting. It felt like I had sung it thousands of times. I woke up and wrote the words down on a pad:

And through the Eyes of God,

I have learned to see

that I am everything and

everything is me.

And through the Breath of God,

I have learned to breathe.

And I am everything and everything is me.

I remember wrestling with sharing this song with the world. The word God definitely was triggering me and brought back everything I had questioned about organized religion. I could still hear my persistent inner voice arguing, "It's a nice song, but it's not going on my record." I then heard an inner voice respond, "No, *it is your record*!" After sitting with it for a while, I thought, it is quite difficult to put a word to the connection that we experience beyond ourselves. The connection to something more than us . . . what we call it is not as important as the connection that we experience.

This is what joins us and cannot separate us. I thought, *If that is the case, then I am good with calling that God.*

Albert Einstein puts it eloquently: "That deep emotional conviction of the presence of a superior reasoning power, which is revealed in the incomprehensible universe, forms my idea of God." This song was a messenger to my soul so that it may truly know that there is no separation. I was guided to pass this message on to anyone who would listen, so now I am passing it on to you in the hope that it will inspire your creative process.

Up until that dream, I thought that I wrote my own songs. It is with this song that I realized one of the main purposes of music is to expand and deepen our spiritual connection. This dream set the knowing that all songs could be divine collaborations—all creation could be. We simply have to invite God in and allow the message to be received by the soul.

The following powerful steps will allow music, sound, and vibration to support and inspire you in creating your own divine collaborations!

Five Steps for Utilizing Music to Enhance Your Creative Process

Step 1: Make Time to Create

Before you even start your creative process, it is important to create *time* for it. Even if it's just a short period of time, when you deem that time sacred you will be amazed by the quality and quantity of what can be created.

I remember when I was moving into the process of creating an album and was given a shorter deadline than expected. I had to reevaluate my creative process and how time related to it. Normally, my process involved five-hour recording sessions, but that would be impossible with the deadline I was given. It was time to shift my belief system that I needed a large block of time to be creative. What I realized was that it wasn't necessarily about the *amount* of time I allotted, but more about *enhancing the quality* of the time I had. Even if I only had five minutes to create, I started to look at those five minutes as a sacred gift from the universe.

Many times we sabotage the actual time we have because we are stressed, not in the mood, or cannot shift our emotions to the necessary state to create. When we deem something sacred, we are announcing to the universe that we are aligning to our divine connection and our creative energy opens up and begins to flow.

To make any time a sacred time, begin by carving out small periods of time in your schedule to create. Anywhere from five minutes to half an hour in the morning, after lunch, and/or before sleep is a great start.

Now, let's make the experience more sacred with music. Choose a song that supports your creative energy. If you don't have a particular song in mind for this exercise, I'd suggest "Sacred Space" by Llewellyn. I love the way the mysterious flutes invite you into the song and the light wind chimes bring in the sense of a gentle breeze to caress the creative process. The important thing is to play a piece of music that will assist in opening and connecting you to your heart, something that speaks to you. The creative process is one that bridges the emotions of the heart and the imagination of the mind.

Get comfortable, and listen to your song, placing your hands on your heart. Feel the energy of your heart and mind connecting. Allow yourself to take these moments to establish the connection between your mind and heart and to strengthen that connection to bring you to your highest creativity. When the song finishes, breathe in through your heart and out through your heart one last time before moving on.

You will notice that once you carve these small amounts of time into your daily practice, you begin to find even more time to create when you least expect it. The ideas begin to flow while you are stuck in traffic, waiting to be seated at a restaurant, doing dishes, or waiting in the doctor's office.

Step 2: Shift Your Environment

Do you have a space that feels conducive to creating? When you look around, do you feel safe and serene? These feelings set the space to be inspired. Does the room feel constrictive or expansive to your creative process? Your environment is a chalice for your creative energy, so it should feel sacred, just like your creative process.

Music is one of the most powerful ways to instantly shift the energy of a physical space. Have you ever walked into a spa and noticed how the music invites you into the environment? It is almost as if your body and mind takes a sigh when you enter and you relax. The environment you create in can have the same effect. I suggest using the song "Sacred Space" by Douglas Blue Feather to help you encourage more sacredness in your space. The beautiful Native American flutes, gentle bell chimes, luring melodies, and wide range of grounding and ethereal tones work well to clear a space.

In addition to using music to clear a space, we can use sound and vibration as well. Sound does a great job of breaking up stagnant, heavy, or negative energy in a room. If you have a hand drum, the lower frequencies of the drum work well with clearing energy in a space. Start by working with the larger areas of the room first and begin to drum into areas that feel heavy. For smaller areas, shakers and striking high frequency tuning forks can fine-tune the energy of the room. Use your intuition, and if the room is still feeling stagnant, repeat the process until you notice a change that is conducive to your creation.

If you don't have a drum or tuning fork I recommend the song "Drum Circle" by Wasichu, which incorporates vibrant and passionate drums with a wide frequency range. There is a powerful intensity that builds within this piece that helps dissolve heavy energy.

Step 3: Meditate with Music

As we move into the pure state of creation we begin to refill our bodies with rejuvenating energy. If you are in a state of stress, your vessel is probably already full—but not with rejuvenating energy. Rather, it's full of your days' events, deadlines, challenges, and mind chatter. Meditation is a wonderful way to empty your vessel and transform your deadlines to lifelines, your challenges to triumphs, and your mind chatter to intuition.

When choosing music for meditation, I usually use instrumental music or music with chants. As your heart entrains with the compositions and you relax, your brain shifts. These slower brain wave states are where we find ourselves "drifting" or daydreaming. It is from this very frame of mind that we spark amazing ideas that seem to come out of nowhere.

Allow yourself to meditate for a few minutes to reinforce opening your pathway to creation. Try this song for starters: "Deep Theta 6 Hz, Part 8" by Steven Halpern.

Step 4: Free Fall with Music

Now that you feel lighter and have room to fill your vessel with new creative energy, it is time for the free fall process. Be prepared to jot down your amazing ideas.

To free fall into your process, put on Constance Demby's "Haven of Peace" or choose your own music to stimulate creativity, and get ready to write. You may wish to ask a question, as this can spark deeper and higher levels of creativity. I like to start off by asking, "What do I need to know about the creation of X (my project)?" This starts the process by asking for information I might not personally have and taps into the infinite field beyond for the answers.

Then, open up the faucet of ideas and let your thoughts flow! Write them down as they occur to you. The important thing is to allow a free flow of ideas. As your words begin to manifest in written form, don't stop to judge or edit them. There is no right or wrong; you are just allowing creation to move through you. Be open to receiving intuitive guidance.

If you feel like you are moving into your mental thought process and constricting the energy, then you can stop or meditate and restart.

When the song has finished, stop. Or, if you still feel like your energy is expansive and your connection is open when the song ends, continue to write.

When you feel your session is complete, use another song to help you ground in the energy of creative flow. You might try my song, "Hallelujah Amen." Music with low drums or more bass usually assists in grounding because we can actually feel those frequencies in our body, not just hear them.

Whether it is for five minutes or five hours, whether you are writing a book, painting, or updating your résumé, every free falling session is productive. Even if your idea has not fully blossomed in the first free fall session, it is seeded. You can bring in the same creative energy to fine-tune and edit your free fall session at any time. This process can a be used for painting, sculpting, writing song lyrics, drafting a business plan, planning a party, or plotting a brand new career . . . anything you want to create!

Step 5: Move Through Creative Blocks

There are times when we may experience a dead end in our creative process but still have the desire to continue. When this happens, you can use all of the techniques we have previously discussed to help you move through creative blocks. To recap, these techniques are:

- Heart Song Breathing Process

- Chanting

- Balancing your energy centers

You can also break through blocks by taking a five-minute dance break. Choose a piece of music from your inspirational playlist or one of the sample playlists listed in the back of the book. Stand up, move, and groove. Shake your body and have fun. Moving stagnant energy will reopen your creative flow, and listening to someone else's musical creation can reignite your creative juices!

If you are a musician yourself, you can also play an instrument to help you break through creative blocks. I can speak from personal experience that there is nothing like playing a musical instrument (your voice is also a musical instrument) to relieve stress and move through creative blocks. Granted, there is a learning curve to get started—but once you do, it is well worth your time. Playing an instrument engages all four of your bodies.

In addition, playing an instrument can also be a beautiful spiritual experience. Those moments when we go to "the zone" and are deeply connected to something beyond ourselves help us to move through creative blocks. When we allow ourselves to improvise and let the music come through us, we are able to tap into a unified field of sound, vibration, and music.

There have been many times I have picked up my guitar when experiencing a creative block and just started playing. Moments later, I experienced new sparks of creative energy and the block was gone! The good news is that you are never too old to pick up a new musical talent. In fact, science shows that one of the best ways to keep your memory sharp is to learn a new musical instrument.

Sometimes the best way to move through a creative block is

collaboration. Remember the age-old saying "Two heads are better than one"? It holds true—especially when it comes to creativity. Two hearts are also better than one! When we combine the knowledge of the brain with the wisdom of the heart we can create anything. The combined idea moves beyond any concept each individual could have created on his or her own.

I have had many experiences when bringing someone in to collaborate on a song brought it from a good song to a great song. When we combined our harmonious heart energy, it created something truly unique. This is true synergy. I'm not sure who created the term "heartstorming," but I think it perfectly describes the method of tapping into the heart's energy in the creative process.

Bringing something into existence can be one of the most amazing adventures we can have in our lifetime. As we create, we are in a high vibrational state, elevating our emotions and our consciousness to collaborate with the ultimate creator in the process. Treat each creation as a sacred journey, and allow music, sound, and vibration to amplify your creative process.

Sound Tools for Transformation

Here are some powerful suggestions for implementing some of this chapter's concepts to create transformation in your life right now.

- Set aside a certain amount of time today to create and clear a physical space that is conducive to your creative process.

- If you feel like you are experiencing a creative block, try one of the creative block-busters we explored in this chapter, such as collaborating with a friend.

- Nurture an idea that has been on the backburner and apply some of the concepts in this chapter to move the idea into physicality.

Suggested Music

The following songs are described in detail within this chapter and are highly recommended for your creative process!

- "Through the Eyes of God" by Barry Goldstein

- "Sacred Space" by Llewellyn

- "Drum Circle" by Wasichu

- "Deep Theta 6 Hz, Part 8" by Steven Halpern

- "Haven of Peace" by Constance Demby

- "Hallelujah Amen" by Barry Goldstein

11

Create Your Ultimate Day Every Day with Music

To me, the concept of distance is not important. Distance doesn't exist, in fact, and neither does time. Vibrations from love or music can be felt everywhere, at all times.

—Yoko Ono

In my experience, when we start a new program of any kind in small intervals on a consistent basis, we build momentum and bring in new positive habits. These small time commitments can create an enormous shift in your being.

The three most important times of your day to incorporate music are:

1. The beginning of your day after you wake up

2. The middle of your day

3. The end of your day before you go to sleep

Beginning Your Day with Music

Before your mind starts running in the morning with your to-do lists, it is important to utilize a piece of music that will set the energy of your day. Determine where you are emotionally in the moment, where you want to go, and what song will be the vibrational match to take you there.

I always look at my morning song as musical nourishment for the beginning of the day. Just like breakfast breaks the fast of not having eaten during your sleep cycle, your morning song breaks the silence of being the first music you hear for the day. Ask yourself, "What piece of music will feed my soul and set the vibration of my day?" Just like your breakfast, the songs can be different every day, depending on where you are emotionally. Remember, music is a bridge that takes you from one state to another, and it can also support and expand your current positive state.

Pick a song or piece of music that reflects or harmonizes with your intention for the day. You can use one of the sample songs in the back of the book, or choose your own. The process for this is simple. Play the song, place your hands on your heart, and allow the music to do what it does best: integrate or spark the energy of your intention for the day.

Starting your day in this way generates a beautiful vibratory field that surrounds you. You become that person who draws curious attention when you walk into a room. You begin to create attraction patterns based on the vibration you radiate. Doing this every day assists in releasing older belief systems and heavy emotions and re-attunes you to your brilliant potential!

Make the beginning of your day a sacred time, the defining moment when you connect with the Divine to reinvent your day every day.

Music and Sound Tools for Midday Rejuvenation

Have you ever seen a commercial for a pharmaceutical drug? There's usually a scene with children playing in a park or a couple walking on a beach while a narrator lists numerous side effects of the drug. Listen to the music. . . . It is usually playful, whimsical, or serene to distract us from the stressful side effects. This is not an accident. We can apply this lesson in a productive way and make music a positive distraction from stress to regroup, re-center, rejuvenate, and reconnect.

A great analogy for using music, sound, and vibration in your midday is comparing your midday music to lunch. Usually by midday most of us have experienced some stressors that have taken us out of the beautiful space we started our morning with. Just as you take a lunch break to replenish and nourish yourself, your musical selections and sound tools should do the same. Following are some fast, simple, and yet powerful ways to reduce your midday stressors with music.

Come Home to Your Heart

If you find yourself in a contracted, stressful state, take a few minutes and connect to your inner music: your heartbeat, your breath, and your sigh. Very often we take on the energy of different people or challenging situations that have occurred during our day. A great way to clear the stresses of the day is to practice the Heart Song Breathing Process for several rounds. No matter what is going on in your day, no one can take away your unique sound signature that exists within. When you connect with your inner music and incorporate it into your daily program, you will never wander far from home. Your heartbeat, your breath, and your sigh are your anchors to reconnecting with your unique vibration and your vital life-force.

Engage Your Brain

Take a few minutes and sing with your favorite song or drum along with it. Engaging your brain in a less analytical way with music gives you the ability to refresh and rejuvenate yourself!

Musical Stress Blaster

Take five minutes to close your eyes and relax or meditate with a calming piece of music from the playlists you have created or from one of the sample playlists provided. Allow yourself to surrender to the music and consciously slow your breath down. As you move to a more peaceful state, look for something that you are grateful for in the moment, and focus on that sense of gratitude to soothe your stress away. Another possibility is listening to a more upbeat, fun, or motivational song to spark and revitalize your energy.

The astounding thing is that we have the capability of re-tuning our day before it turns into an emotional rollercoaster. It's all about awareness. Listening to music is a sacred privilege and a blessing, a power tool in building the foundation to a harmonious life. Once we learn to red flag ourselves, we can stop magnifying stressful situations by implementing music and sound tools in our midday to bring us back to our original morning intentions.

Winding Down with Music

When we utilize music to regulate our sleeping patterns, it becomes a call or signal to the core of our spirit that it is time to wind down and move from the excitement of the day into the sacredness of night. I would suggest utilizing a piece of music at about 60 bpm (one beat every second), the rate of music that can entrain your heart to a relaxed state, as you'll remember from earlier. Your heart and brain can entrain to this relaxed state and bridge you into a more conducive physical, mental, emotional, and spiritual state to move into restful sleep. About an hour before you go to sleep every night, utilize a very peaceful piece of music to cleanse and reset with.

Just as Pavlov conditioned his dogs to anticipate food by hearing the sound of a bell, we can condition ourselves to anticipate sleep with the sound of music to make our nights more sacred. As we hear the music, we let out a sigh and surrender all that is not in our control to a higher power. You may be looking for a way to calm the household down. This practice of having music playing can be a great way of winding down together. Your kids will start to identify the winding down process with the music. When we can train our four bodies to relax at an early age, we create better sleep habits and have less stress and anxiety as adults.

In addition to listening to music at 60 beats per minute, some criteria that I have found to be beneficial:

- *Listen to music with long tones*—When tones or notes are sustained there is less movement musically and less for your mind to interpret. There is an underlying rhythm that creates a flow, but it is not percussive. It is similar to the flow of a tide that gently cascades its way up to the sands of the beach and smoothly rejoins its original source. Music with long tones can create this same gentle ebb and flow.

- *Select music with limited melodies*—Melody engages the mind's judgment system. As we hear a melody we move through a decision-making process. We also perceive the outcome of a melody, and anticipate its next note, making it harder to sleep.

- *Avoid music that triggers emotions*—Different musical pieces can trigger various emotions. When the music remains neutral, it allows the listener to have his or her own experience. The intention of relaxation music before bedtime is that it creates a relaxing environment without distraction.

Imagine definitively becoming the DJ of your life and programming your day with music, sound, and vibration to assist in getting prepared for corporate meetings, challenging family situations, or life celebrations. In addition to these three key times for integrating music, you can work music into your day in much smaller intervals, wherever your schedule might allow.

Making music part of your daily schedule is truly the start to creating a transformation. You may be surprised to find just how many amazing beneficial effects this daily musical practice will yield in terms of your quality of life and improved health.

Sound Tools for Transformation

Here are some powerful suggestions for implementing some of this chapter's concepts to create transformation in your life right now.

- We usually spend so much time creating lists of things to *do* that we forget about our list of things to *be*. I invite you to compose a Things to Be list for your day. Here's an example:

Today I will be kind.

Today I will be courageous.

Today I will be loving.

Today I will be patient.

This helps to set the tone for how your day can blossom by speaking and listening to your heart!

- Prepare three songs for tomorrow that you will use for morning, afternoon, and evening. Have them ready so there is no room for excuses. Think of these songs as you would a meal: Your morning song is like breakfast. Utilize your afternoon song like a lunch break. Treat your evening song like dessert after dinner. Allow music to nourish your soul today and every day. As you nourish, you build strength and anchor in this way of being!

- Begin to plug in some of the vibrational tools in your day as needed to manage stress, transform negative emotions, and improve your physical well-being. Use the Heart Song Breathing Process when stress seems too tough to bear. I also recommend balancing the energy centers through toning, songs, and intention as an excellent complement to your morning and pre-bed musical rituals.

Suggested Music

- For morning: "Morning Has Broken" by Cat Stevens—This song takes you on a magnificent journey back to being thankful for the day that is ahead of you and the miraculous gifts that nature provides.

- For midday: "I'm So Excited" by The Pointer Sisters—If motivation or a jumpstart is what you need midday, this relentlessly upbeat song is the perfect spark to reignite you!

- For evening: "Cosmic Consciousness" by Barry Goldstein—Imagine yourself floating in space and letting go of your physical body to reach a very deep, relaxed state before sleep. This composition perfectly supports the suggested criteria for sleep music.

12

Conclusion

So now the secret is out ... Music, sound, and vibration are the secret language of the heart. Music has been speaking to you your whole life, but I hope after reading this book it speaks to you in a much different and more profound way. A way in which you are active, aware, and empowered in knowing that this language is a two-way conversation.

As you implement a daily music practice, you begin to speak to your heart and listen to find more subtle guidance. A daily practice of working with your breath and heartbeat tells your heart you are thankful for each moment. Chanting or using a mantra in the middle of your day tells your heart it is time to move from your head and into your heart. Singing or listening with songs from your playlist can shift negative emotions that you have carried your whole life and create powerful and heartfelt transformation. You have the ability to shift your moments, your days, and your life with the music and sound tools provided to improve your health and overall quality of life.

When there are times you feel lost or are having a hard time understanding certain aspects of your life, take that long but beautiful journey from your head to your heart and let music be the translator. Then listen . . . You will notice that by applying the methods in this book you can go past just listening from the analytical mind and tap into the intuitive heart. You allow yourself to make decisions from a place of knowing, trust, and compassion.

As your life changes through this deepened relationship with your heart, you become more compassionate to yourself, to others, and to the world.

Join me in the exciting final section, which will provide musical prescriptions for specific health conditions!

PART THREE

Musical Prescriptions *for* Health

Music as Medicine

In our exploration of music's medicinal properties, we have shown that healing is not just something that happens in the physical body alone. When we heal emotionally, mentally, and spiritually, it affects our physical health as well. Only when we address all four aspects of our health can we come back to being whole and truly be healed. The research cited in this section provides solid evidence that music can benefit all four bodies!

We are living in exciting times where science and spirituality are being bridged. The role of music, sound, and vibration in this process are integral. Many of us want to take the benefits of music, sound, and vibration into more mainstream areas such as corporations, hospitals, hospices, medical practices, and the private sector. Having good, solid research creates a more grounded approach to make this happen. The studies I have referenced lead the way for you to delve deeper into the science and determine if the findings resonate with you. Take the journey. Then share the experience and inspire others to do the same.

I have also provided testimonials of how music has benefited specific medical conditions. There are suggested musical and vibrational prescriptions based on my experience in the field, and I cite organizations that provide additional expertise and resources to put it all into action.

Remember, none of these prescriptions are intended to replace your current medications or medical treatment plans, although some might have the power to! They are meant to provide strong support in your journey to optimal health. The conditions are presented in alphabetical order.

Let's get started on uncovering some amazing findings utilizing music for treating specific conditions! I have added an abbreviated contents page for this section to help you find the ailment you are looking for quickly.

Alzheimer's Disease

The Alzheimer's Association projects that the United States will see the number of Alzheimer's cases increase by 40 percent from 2015 to 2025. One of the greatest fears of American adults is the loss of memory. With these startling statistics, focus on treating and managing the negative symptoms of Alzheimer's disease is crucial. This disease touches not only the person directly diagnosed, but also his or her family and friends, who in most cases watch the person's quality of life deteriorate day by day. Insomnia is one of the most frequent negative symptoms of Alzheimer's for the patient and caregivers.

The use of both music and music therapy shows amazing results in Alzheimer's patients. The difference between the terms "music" and "music therapy" used here is that "music" means the music itself provides the benefit, while "music therapy" indicates that the relationship between the music therapist and the patient, and also a specific music process that the patient is involved in (such as singing), provides the benefit.

Research demonstrates that melatonin (a hormone best known for regulating sleep cycles) increased in a four-week music therapy program with Alzheimer's patients.[19]

In addition, adding stimulating and familiar background music to Alzheimer's patient's environments increased positive behaviors (calmness, relaxation, etc.) while decreasing negative behaviors (aggression, anxiety, etc.).[20]

As we saw in the example of Henry in chapter 3, an Alzheimer's patient, patients have also been able to recall more personal memories after listening to music that related specifically to their lives.

Musical Prescription

If you are looking to assist someone with Alzheimer's using music, find out what type of music he or she enjoys or has previously enjoyed. If the person is unable to tell you, see if any friends, relatives, or loved ones can provide more information.

Just as with traditional medicine, the prescription dosage is important. Start out with three or four songs played at various intervals during the day, as tolerated. Play the music at a low volume that will be comfortable. Fine-tune the playlist based on his or her reaction. If there is a song that the person doesn't like or that triggers negative emotions or behaviors, replace it with another one. Watching *Alive Inside*, the movie that chronicles the Alzheimer's patient Henry, can also be really helpful.

If someone in your life is affected by Alzheimer's, you know it can be devastating. For caretakers, affirmations are a way to voice and release the anxiety of a situation and transform it into a more positive emotion. Preparing yourself with a thirty-second affirmation can transform a potentially negative visit into a bonding experience on another level. Remember, words carry vibration, so before going to see the patient, place your hands on your heart and use this affirmation if it resonates with you. (Feel free to substitute the words in bold italic to make it more specific to your situation.)

> *I recognize the **breath and heartbeat** within **Mom** and appreciate who **she** is in this moment. I see beyond the **anger** and cherish her **sense of humor** within.*

Suggested Music

"The Summer Wind" by Frank Sinatra—That big band sound has been utilized with Alzheimer's patients to evoke positive memories—and who better to try than Frank Sinatra?

Attention Deficit Hyperactivity Disorder (ADHD)

Attention deficit hyperactivity disorder (ADHD) is defined by inattention, impulsivity, and/or hyperactivity. Research indicates that music can increase the production of dopamine, a messenger chemical produced in the brain (that can be deficient in many ADHD sufferers) that works with attention, memory, and motivation with no harmful side effects.[21]

Musical Prescription

Listen to music that provides a strong sense of rhythm. It can assist in providing a focal point. Allow the person with ADHD to choose his or her own music whenever possible. If you are working with someone who chooses music that is not your typical taste, stay open to the possibility that it may still be helpful. Pop songs offer a sense of structure with verses, choruses, bridges, and endings. Strong choruses create the feeling of knowing what is coming next. This can provide an invitation for participation and help to release unfocused energy.

Suggested Music

"Just the Way You Are" by Bruno Mars—I suggest this song because it has very distinct sections that the listener can focus on. In addition, the positive message of not having to change who you are to be amazing is a powerful message for people who have this disorder.

For winding down at bedtime, utilize more relaxing, calming music. I recommend "Adagio for Sleep" by Liquid Mind. The angelic opening chords and long, peaceful tones of this piece invite the mind to surrender. It gently leads the listener to make a seamless transition from the mind busyness of the day into winding down to a more serene state for the evening.

Autism

Autism can impair a person's ability to regulate, understand, and communicate his or her emotions. The use of traditional language can be limiting when trying to express emotion. Music, on the other hand, can access an array of emotions even without using words. Research points out that music is an alternative way for people with autism to access and communicate their emotions with less difficulty.[22]

Once someone has had an experience and new connection to emotional understanding through music, he or she has an anchor for future emotional understanding to occur.

Over the last ten years, I have received many testimonials from people who have utilized my music to benefit clients or patients with autism. I pass these on in the hope that they will be of benefit to you.

From Frustration to Hugs

Recently I was working with an eleven-year-old autistic boy. We were trying to recreate situations that create frustration and subsequent "meltdowns." When I asked him why he wasn't feeling frustrated, my client told me that it was the music. I was playing Barry's CD, Home, *in the background.*

My client said he felt it in his brain and ears. I asked him if he knew about chakras. When he said he didn't, I encouraged him to "scan" his body and I took him through the seven chakra areas in his body while suggesting he feel for the music or any other sensations deep inside, yet not where the organs are. He pointed to the areas corresponding to the solar

*plexus and abdominal chakras and said he felt a
"thrumming" that calmed him. I suggested that
maybe the music connected the physical (brain, ears)
with the inner (upper and lower abdomen) and he
agreed. He looked so peaceful! He then suggested
he was finished, and when he left he gave me three
separate long, full hugs.*

—Judy Lipson, MA, LPC

Play It All Day

*I work with children who have disabilities, many
of them severe. I find that the Ambiology 5: Eden
CD is very helpful with my autistic and emotionally
disabled children. They actually are learning to
relax with its help.*

*One of my autistic, emotionally disturbed students
usually vehemently dislikes music. He covers his ears
with his hands, screams, and cries when he hears it.
He is, however, actually asking me specifically for the
Eden CD and wants it to be played all day!*

—Willa Ficarra, speech-language therapist

Musical Prescription

Autism is a spectrum disorder. Choose music that is simple for severe cases, and more complex and variable music for mild to moderate cases.[23]

Cater the music to the person's tastes. If possible, try to make him or her part of the process to find favorite songs and genres. Start with lower volume levels and work your way up gradually.

You might find that the person you are working with is more sensitive to specific frequencies. In my experience, pieces of music with a lot of bass (low) or treble (high) sounds may be disturbing. Play all music in small increments to test his or her initial response. Slowly increase the duration of the music if there is a positive response.

If you are looking to increase his or her emotional understanding through music, pick a song that symbolizes the emotion of being happy and another that symbolizes being sad. Use this as a starting point for music as a translator of emotions.

Suggested Music

For translating emotions into music, try using the songs below to represent the feelings of happiness and sadness respectively:

- "Happy" by Pharrell Williams

- "Symphony No. 6 in B Minor" by Tchaikovsky

- *Light from Assisi* by Richard Shulman to create calmness

- Bonus for caretakers: "So It Goes" from the Songs for Autism campaign, which paints a touching picture of those affected by autism and their loved ones.

Bereavement and Grief

Losing a loved one can be one of the most spiritually challenging situations we experience. I know that music was an enormous help for me when my dad passed. At my father's funeral I sang a song I had previously written for him. It provided a way for me to release the grief I was feeling from the loss. The song was called "Hey Daddy," and it expressed the regret of not knowing the little things about my dad that I had never asked. It also created an intimacy at the funeral that was touching and comforting for all that attended.

At times, music can support us in expressing our grief, and other times it can act as a pausing mechanism to allow us to rest and rejuvenate from a very emotionally draining process. Paying tribute to the person who has passed through music and song can be a very powerful and beneficial process.

Musical Prescription

Create your own ceremony utilizing music, sound, and vibration to honor the person who has passed. Choose a song that assists you in remembering that person and that speaks of his or her qualities—a song you know he or she loved or one that held a connection between the two of you.

Set your environment to make it feel special, or choose a significant place. Before playing the song, place your hand on your heart and gently breathe in and out. Be thankful for your vital heartbeat and breath. As you play the song, thank the person for the ways he or she touched your life. Know that you can still entrain with the essence of that person although his or her physical body is no longer here. Allow your feelings to flow. The sound of crying is a powerful vehicle for releasing and transforming grief. As you honor this person, you also honor yourself and the relationship that was shared between you.

If you feel you need more help, professional musical therapy is another excellent way to process loss.

Songwriting, lyric writing, singing in a group, and playing instruments together can assist in releasing and moving through emotions. It's not about being a professional musician, it's about using the process as a tool to explore, release, and transform grief.

Suggested Music

"Europa (Earth's Cry Heaven's Smile)" by Carlos Santana is one of the most emotional guitar instrumentals you will ever listen to. The song starts off very gently and brings in a sense of safety that allows for surrender. As the guitar sustains and "cries," the percussion sways and orbits around the guitar and gives the listener a sense of permission to release grief and connect with more expansive and heavenly energies. A very powerful piece!

Cancer

The American Cancer Society estimates that more than 1.6 million people will be diagnosed with cancer in 2016. Finding ways to treat anxiety and pain and improve quality of life for this devastating disease are very important. The fact that music is noninvasive, low-cost, has no negative side effects, and does not interfere with medical treatment is a huge factor in considering and creating a consistent music program for cancer patients.

According to the American Cancer Society, "New research supports listening to recorded music, as well as music therapy, to improve anxiety, pain, mood, quality of life, heart rate, respiratory rate, and blood pressure in cancer patients." In addition, research has demonstrated that utilizing music during high-dose chemotherapy can lessen nausea and vomiting.[24]

From the stages of being diagnosed with cancer to cancer recovery, many mental challenges can occur that affect our brain health and overall quality of life, including anxiety, stress, and depression. Research suggests that choral singing may improve quality of life and depression in cancer survivors.[25]

Music for cancer patients can be used in various ways. Kristine Salmon, an integrative oncology and wellness senior manager, began utilizing my music with her cancer clients at Banner MD Anderson Cancer Center in Arizona.

> *The patient was able to let go of muscular tension and stress for an hour, and that rejuvenated her body! She had been struggling with cancer-related fatigue for nearly a year. To me, this was beautiful, and I am truly grateful to Barry and his music for aiding the patient in experiencing energy again!*

In addition to addressing physical symptoms, music can assist in creating a more balanced, stress-free environment where the physical body can repair and the emotional and mental bodies can rest. It can also inspire a stronger sense of spiritual well-being and allow us to deepen our connection with something outside ourselves and beyond our health challenges.

Musical Prescription

If you are receiving treatments that might require a lot of physical energy, pick a piece of music in the morning that will inspire you and lift your energy emotionally. As we have shown throughout this book, keeping your emotions positive can affect your physical body beneficially.

During and after treatments, or on days you are not receiving treatments, pick music that will relax and rejuvenate you. Just allow and surrender when listening and your body will move into the parasympathetic relaxed state in which rejuvenation, repair, and detoxification can occur.

Take a walk in nature. Nature is a part of the language of music, and not only does it speak to us, it can act as a lifeline and coping strategy.

Suggested Music

- "This Little Light of Mine" by Faith Rivera—A wonderful, fun, and funky rendition of a childhood song that is perfect for lifting the mood and invites listeners to let their inner light shine.

- "Something More" by Nick Vujicic—This inspirational song and video helps to put any illness into perspective seeing the trials and tribulations that the artist has conquered.

- "Silk Road" by Kitaro—The exotic flutes, nature sounds, and percolating bells make this a perfect piece of music for rejuvenation and relaxation.

Cardiovascular Conditions

Heart problems are a common medical ailment in this day and age. In addition to entraining your heart to a coherent state, music can also assist those who have more extensive cardiovascular problems that may even require surgery. For example, research indicates that listening to relaxing music after open-heart surgery can decrease levels of stress and increase levels of oxytocin, a hormone that can improve our emotions.[26]

Additionally, research has uncovered that different types of music, such as classical music and meditation music, have had the greatest benefit to our cardiovascular health.[27]

Musical Prescription

Utilize a piece of music that brings you to a state of joy at least once a day. Studies reveal that joyful music can promote vascular health.[28]

Select a piece of music that evokes gratitude and peacefulness to calm yourself down in stressful times during your day, to help lower your blood pressure, and to keep your heart healthy. Connect with your heart on a daily basis. Use the Heart Song Breathing Process. Creating a daily practice of this can help transform stress and anxiety and may also help regulate your heartbeat and lower your blood pressure.

If you are going into heart surgery, utilize relaxing music before, during, and after the operation. Don't forget that you want your surgeon in a focused and relaxed state as well. Ask for the music to be played for you and your medical team.

Suggested Music

- "Happy Together" by The Turtles—This classic rock song is an antidote to negative feelings and creates an invitation to feel joyous.

- "Om Shree Saché" by Deva Premal—The perfect piece of peaceful music to calm yourself down in stressful times during your day.

- *Watermark* by Enya—This album sets the perfect space for a focused yet relaxed environment in the operating room.

Dementia

Alzheimer's Disease International reports that worldwide, an estimated 46.8 million people are living with some form of dementia. Symptoms of dementia include negative emotions, memory problems, sleep disturbances, and agitated behavior. Multiple studies have found that music therapy and music have been beneficial in reducing agitated behaviors.[29]

Serenity in Harlem

In 2003, Phil Veneziano approached me and asked if I could suggest any of my music that might help his mom who was suffering from dementia. Phil had taken on the role of caretaker in his noisy apartment in Harlem, and his mom was having trouble getting to sleep at night. Insomnia is one of the most treatment-resistant symptoms of dementia. I suggested that Phil try *Ambiology 5: Eden*. Phil later shared with me that the music provided a "sonic cushion" from the street sounds, and that his mother had become so accustomed to the CD that she would insist that it was put on every evening as she prepared for bed, even when the streets were quiet.

Phil shared his story with me from a deep place of gratitude:

> *She was frightened and tense most of the time,*
> *wondering what the future had in store for her.*
> *But when I put "her music" on, as she called it, she*
> *would close her eyes and drift into a comfortable,*
> *deep sleep. It was her moment of tranquility in a*
> *very trying time. As I would leave the room after*
> *I turned on "her music," I could see a faint smile*
> *on Mom's face as the opening chords sounded. She*
> *seemed to know that she would soon be in a comfort-*
> *able place, and I can't express to you how relieved*
> *that made me feel after all she'd been through.*

Musical Prescription

The Alzheimer's Association has an excellent protocol for utilizing music with dementia: identify music that is familiar and enjoyable to the person. If possible, let him or her choose the music.

Choose a source of music that isn't interrupted by commercials, which can cause confusion.

Use music to create the mood you want. For example, a tranquil piece of music can help create a calm environment, while a faster-paced song from someone's childhood may boost his or her spirit and evoke happy memories.

Avoid sensory overload; eliminate competing noises by shutting windows and doors and turning off the television. Make sure the volume of the music is not too loud.[30]

Suggested Music

"The Secret Garden" by Diane Arkenstone—This song is seeded in beauty and gently blossoms into a sacred journey that takes the listener, whether caretaker or patient, into a safe and nurturing environment.

Dental Pain and Anxiety

Music can play an important role in making a dental procedure that is a not-so-pleasant experience into a much more tolerable one. Music allows our bodies to move into a relaxed state and in some cases even reduce the amount of pain and anxiety experienced.[31]

One client of mine shared an experience in which she had a dental emergency and ended up being treated by a local dentist who had a reputation for being rough with his patients. While sitting in the chair waiting for the hygienist, she realized she had her music player with her and quickly put on some uplifting and heart-opening music. She had always associated this music with a place of comfort and familiarity, like home, so when she began to listen to the music her mind returned to that state of joy and relaxation. This allowed her to get through what she described as her "brutal" dentist appointment far more easily than she ever imagined would be possible.

Musical Prescription

Listen to relaxation music while in the waiting room. Much of your anxiety can be created in this stage while anticipating the procedure. Bring a set of comfortable headphones and set your volume level so that it is loud enough to block out some of the external noises but soft enough to keep you in a relaxed state while in the chair. Breathe with the music and keep your eyes closed during the process if possible. Allow yourself to entrain with the music, and let yourself move into a more relaxed brain wave state, such as alpha or theta.

Suggested Music

"Dolphin Dreams" by Jonathan Goldman—This remarkable piece transports you to a sonic sanctuary with the use of nature sounds, beautiful tones, and textures.

Depression

The Centers for Disease Control and Prevention (CDC) reports that 9 percent of Americans are affected by depression, and many are not receiving specific treatment. The number of patients diagnosed increases about 20 percent every year. Music is a highly accepted art form that most people have access to at little to no cost. It makes complete sense to utilize many of the tools described in this book to combat depression. If you or a loved one is battling depression, the following prescriptions will give you some easy ideas to plug in.

Musical Prescription

If you are feeling depressed, meet yourself where you are. Use the Heart Song Breathing Process to pinpoint what emotion might be contributing to your depression and what emotion you would like to go to, and then create an "Antidepressant" playlist with songs that can elevate your emotions.

Remember, words carry meaning. Listen to your inner voice and monitor your negative thoughts. Start each day with a morning song and an intention for your day that lifts you.

Sing along with your favorite music! Research has indicated that singing helps to combat depression, especially in older people.[32]

Suggested Music

"O-o-h Child" by The Five Stairsteps—It's hard to listen to this song without being affected. There is so much positive energy within this upbeat, inspirational song that we should listen to it once a day and sing with it to combat depression!

Insomnia

Insomnia affects between 50 and 70 million Americans alone. The National Sleep Foundation reports that 48 percent of Americans report occasional insomnia, while 22 percent experience insomnia every night or almost every night. If you are taking your highly active day into your evening and not releasing or processing the events and emotions that occurred, you might as well be driving your fast vehicle into the insomnia lane.

Sleep challenges can sometimes result when our circadian

rhythms are disturbed. Our internal biological clocks regulate our sleep patterns, and music can create the perfect bridge to resetting our circadian rhythms. Studies confirm that soothing music can help you fall asleep faster and get deeper sleep.[33] This supports much of what has been stated in this book: music with a tempo of 60–80 beats per minute, a slow, constant rhythm, low-frequency tones, and calm, relaxing melodies can assist in treating sleep disorders.

Sleeping with a Musician

"Before I set my intention, I want you to know that I sleep with Barry Goldstein every night," said one woman at a workshop I facilitated. The room was filled with laughter. She explained that she used my music to help her fall asleep and to create a state of relaxation that allowed her brain to turn off and rest.

As we went around the circle, it got worse. A husband said, "I don't sleep with Barry Goldstein, but my wife does." It continued around a circle of about thirty people, and by the end I was beet red.

If you would have told me twenty years ago when I was a rock musician, that my music would be putting people to sleep every night, I would have been highly insulted. Now, I consider it the highest compliment.

Musical Prescription

About an hour before you go to sleep every night, as you're starting to wind down, shut off the TV or computer, lower the lights, and turn on your music. Choose a piece of music that will entrain your heart to a relaxed state. As your heart entrains to the music, your brain will follow and your busy mind will start to quiet. Allow the music to fill the room. Let your breathing adapt to the gentle wave of the music. Move beyond listening with your ears and hear it with your heart.

If your sleeping patterns (circadian rhythms) have moved out of sync, it may take a few days or up to a few weeks to reset these rhythms. Used nightly, the music will begin to act as a bridge from your busy day to your winding down at night. Sleep will follow. . . .

Suggested Music

Ambiology 6: Genesis by Barry Goldstein—This CD has proven to be very effective in improving insomnia in many patients that have been diagnosed with insomnia. It's balance of warm, low tones immersed in a lush blanket of sound with minimal melodies makes it a perfect soundtrack to fall asleep to.

Pain

It is well known that the number one reason people seek a doctor is pain. Music can provide a safe, noninvasive, side effect–free therapy for pain reduction. Studies have found that playing music lessens the need for sedation medication, relaxes patients, and reduces pain.[34] They also show that music improved patients' overall experience with their medical procedures. Another study showed increased functional mobility and decreased pain in fibromyalgia patients.[35]

Musical Prescription

Use soothing music to move you into a relaxed state before, during, and after procedures or when you are experiencing any pain. Toning and chanting can be wonderful ways to entrain the brain to more relaxed states, elevate your heart connection, and create a relaxation response in the physical body. In addition, chanting and toning can take the attention away from the pain and anxiety associated with an upcoming procedure. Carve out five minutes in your day to chant or tone.

Utilize your breath, one of your inner soul sounds. Breathe in and out in time with a piece of music that is comfortable for you, and as you release your breath focus on releasing tension in the area where you are experiencing pain.

Suggested Music

- "Illumination Of The Heart" by Deuter—This piece contains beautiful flutes, heavenly textures, and light, earthy rhythms that connect the listener with a beautiful feeling of well-being. Perfect for before or after a procedure, and also a great piece for gentle breath work.

- "Om Shanti" by Rickie Byars Beckwith—The meaning of *shanti* is "peaceful." This song is a call to find peace in the mind and soul. As we chant "Om Shanti," we have the ability to release tension and stress we are holding in our body and transform ourselves into a more peaceful state.

Palliative Care and the Dying Process

The benefit of music in the dying process is just as important as it is in any other life process. Listening to music every day during this process can bring a sense of peace and calmness and can combat feelings of fear, anxiety, and even pain to create a better quality of life for patients.[36]

In addition, the emotional state of the caregivers is an important part of patient care. Music can be an important tool to center and rejuvenate the caretakers so that they may be truly present during this sacred time of transition.

Winnie and the Butterfly

During my private sound healing sessions with Winnie, one of my favorite clients, she commented many times that she had never been so relaxed in all of her ninety years. During these sessions, we were able to release energy and emotions that she had been holding in her body for many years to bring her to a place of unconditional love and preparedness for the next step in her soul's journey.

A few years after I met Winnie, she suffered from congestive heart failure. The last few weeks of her life were frightening for both her and her family, but by listening to my music throughout the day (and night) and during her transition, both she and her family experienced sensations of deep calm, acceptance, and undeniable love.

Winnie's daughter Carol shared the role of music in her mom's life celebration:

> *A little more than three months after Winnie passed, our friends and family celebrated her life at the Nature Center at Copper Mountain Resort, a place that Winnie and Ed spent years hiking and skiing. As we gathered at nearly 11,000 feet on a pristine, bluebird sunny day, Barry sang Winnie's favorite song that he wrote, "Through the Eyes of God," and the attendees were transfixed. As he moved through the lyrics and came to "I am the butterfly's new wings," the wind picked up and a butterfly gracefully flew behind Barry from east to west. The gasp from the audience was audible, for they too recognized the significance of Barry's powerful words and the appearance of Winnie through that butterfly. Mom was very present with us, and she was joyful. Her message came through loud and clear that she was still alive and connected to us from the other side—forever.*

I can still see Winnie's smiling face and feel so blessed and touched to have been part of her life and her transition.

Musical Prescription

Use a serene piece of music that can provide a safe, nurturing environment for the patient, family members, loved ones, and caretakers. Utilize music to encourage deep emotional bonding and interactions to help relieve stress and anxiety. Self-selected music or favorite songs can encourage memories associated with the music and create a peaceful life review and sense of closure.

Suggested Music

Ambiology 4: Home by Barry Goldstein—*Home* is the perfect album for palliative care and transitioning. It is one hour of continuous music that brings the heart to a relaxed state effortlessly. It contains prayer bowls, earthy, low tones, and subtle melodies. The intention that is embedded in this piece is that the listener feels a sense of home regardless of his or her surroundings.

Parkinson's Disease

The Parkinson's Disease Foundation reports an estimated 7–10 percent of people are living in the world with this challenging disease, and music is showing great promise in many areas of treatment.

In a novel study, music therapy was administered to control symptoms and improve quality of life for patients. The study utilized choral singing, voice exercise, and rhythmic and free body movements and showed positive effects on motor improvement and emotional states.[37]

Musical Prescription

Drumming reportedly has great potential to become a new therapy for Parkinson's patients. Research suggests that playing music actually increases serotonin and dopamine production in the brain, chemicals that are depleted by Parkinson's and that decrease more severely with the progression of the disease.[38]

Rhythmic auditory stimulation (RAS) is a method you can utilize with a music therapist that enables Parkinson's patients to find the exact rhythm that supports optimal gait. RAS may positively influence initiating movements, rhythm and symmetry, freezing of gait, coordination, and endurance.[39]

Suggested Music

"Origins" by Glenn Velez—This strong, steady drumming piece incorporates powerful trance-inducing rhythms. A perfect song for Parkinson's patients and their family members to drum along to tap into the benefits of the recommended prescription.

Pregnancy and Childbirth

Bringing a child into the world can be one of the most amazing experiences that we encounter in our lives. Research unveils that incorporating music, sound, and vibration before, during, and after birth has benefits for both the child and the mother. Such studies have found that not only can music be used to lessen pain and anxiety in the mother (and thus in the child) during labor and delivery, but newborns are also capable of recognizing music that was played or sung to them before birth.[40]

Evelyn Simmons, the coordinator of midwifery services at Alivio Medical Center in Chicago, told me that using relaxing music helped to entrain the mother and child's heartbeat and breath to the music, creating a soothing atmosphere even in the midst of painful labor. This shared field of relaxation and calmness that was created between mother and child with the assistance of this music radiated outward and calmed everyone else who was present at the child's birth, making for a miraculous and harmonious entrance into the world!

Evelyn shared a tender but powerful moment from one of many births utilizing music:

> *With each contraction, the power of [the mother's] breath and her heart's rhythm entraining with the music were her path to inner strength. I admired her strength and her ability to rhythmically move through, then the crowning of the beautiful Valentine's Day baby's head, the climactic part of birth. I saw her tap into her inner strength and embrace her freedom from fear. The baby emerged from the womb and at that moment we all felt the holy sacredness of birth. All three of our hearts were connected in one rhythm. It was amazing.*

Musical Prescription

Before birth and during labor, choose music that alleviates stress and puts you in a highly relaxed state. Remember that the mother's stress is also felt by the infant, so the more stress-free she is able to stay, the less it will negatively affect her child.

Utilize gentle, peaceful music as a communication tool from twenty-eight weeks on to provide a tranquil environment for yourself and your unborn child. This is the time period when fetuses respond reliably to music through changes in heart rate and behavior.[41]

Use the same music to bring your child into the world. This can be a calming mechanism during the process to create safety and serenity for you, your child, and the delivery team. You and your child will recognize the music. Play the same music for the child after birth and keep it on low volumes to provide sonic nurturing in the nursery. He or she can recognize it's their song and feel your love through it.

A mother's voice is one of the most precious musical gifts you can give your child. Sing your child lullabies before birth. Welcome him or her into the world with your voice and songs. Let it be the first powerful rite of passage!

Suggested Music

Ambiology 1: The Heart by Barry Goldstein—The relaxing and soothing tempo of this album will help to guide you and your child's hearts to entrain with the music and can help reduce the anxiety, fear, and pain that come along with childbirth. I have received numerous testimonials of its benefits in childbirth.

Psychosis

For many of the conditions in this section, relaxing or calming music has been part of our prescription. But there are some exceptions. Research indicates that relaxing music isn't necessarily beneficial for psychosis. Music has been shown to be effective in suppressing and combating the symptoms of psychosis, but classical music did not prove as effective as non-classical music in reducing these symptoms.[42]

Musical Prescription

Start with the person's preferred music. More musical stimulation may be necessary for fast-paced or agitated brain states. Start to reduce musical stimulation to help calm the person as his or her brain state adapts. The key is meeting the patient where he or she is; then observe and adapt.

Suggested Music

The best music for someone struggling with psychosis is whatever that person 's preferred music is, or music that the caregiver observes to be calming. Follow the musical prescription given above.

Stress

Everyone has heard of the dangers that stress can place not only on the physical body, but on the emotional, spiritual, and mental bodies as well, which is why it is so important to mitigate our stress levels as much as we can. Research indicates that music can be a vital aspect of stress management by reducing stress hormones.[43] Make sure to add music to your daily program to help reduce stress. Give yourself musical interludes during which you can unwind, relax, and release the stress you carry with you throughout your day.

Musical Prescription

We all have stress in our life. It's about how we respond to it. You have the ability to "compose" yourself and guide anxiety and pressure in a different direction. Take a five-minute vacation, surrender and explore. People relieve stress in different ways. Some people love to move and dance, some need to sit still to calm down. Do what feels best for your four bodies, and follow the beat of your inner drum—your heart! It knows what you need in this moment, so don't forget to listen to it.

Suggested Music

- "Stir It Up" by Bob Marley—Take a joyous trip to Jamaica, *sway* to the gentle breeze, and surrender.

- "El Cantante" by Marc Anthony—*Stand up* and *move* to these beautiful Latin salsa rhythms.

- "What the Pipa Says" by Lin Hai & Friends— *Relax* and *float* into this beautiful exotic Chinese instrumental and allow it to wash away your stresses.

Stroke

The World Health Organization reports that approximately 15 million people have strokes each year, 5 million die, and another 5 million are disabled permanently.

According to the National Aphasia Association, 25–40 percent of people who survive a stroke develop a condition known as aphasia, which results from injury or damage to the language parts of the brain and can affect the person's ability to speak, write, and understand language. In some cases a person can still sing but cannot speak.

The curiosity of how music could assist with this issue led to the development of musical intonation therapy, which uses melody and rhythm to engage specific areas of the brain. A promising study indicated that music may be teaching the brain to reorganize itself as discussed in previous chapters. This reorganization seems to support music's ability to help pave the way for speech in stroke patients.[44] In addition, research reports that "piano training can result in sustainable improvements in upper extremity function in chronic stroke survivors."[45]

Musical Prescription

Cognition can be improved through rhythm games, musical performances, and songwriting.[46] Playing a drum can help to improve movement and muscle control in a stroke survivor, and can also enhance the range of motion in the upper extremities. To improve speech and communication, try exercising mouth muscles, rhyming, or chanting and singing words, using these abilities to gain speech improvements.

Suggested Music

Well-known songs that are remembered easily, such as "Happy Birthday" or "Jingle Bells," are a great start because the melodic aspects are already familiar. For songs that provide strong rhythms, encourage the person to clap, stomp his or her feet, or drum along. I recommend "We Will Rock You" by Queen and "Hollaback Girl" by Gwen Stefani, which both have infectious rhythms that encourage participation.

Moving Forward with Musical Prescriptions

There is continuing and exciting new research being reported on utilizing music, sound, and vibration to enhance our physical, mental, emotional, and spiritual health on a daily basis. There are oncologists using singing bowls, scientists studying the frequency of a cat's purr and its relationship to our health, and books on earthing that show the physical benefits of connecting to the earth's vibration. We are living in exciting times!

One of the main intentions of this book is to teach you how to use music as a bridge to help bring together science and spirituality, heart, and mind. Many of the principles and terms can be applied to transforming our life situations, manifesting our highest intentions, and leading a healthy and fruitful life. One of the best things about learning the building blocks and basics about music and how it relates to the health of your four bodies is that you now have a foundation to build your own musical health practice.

Remember, ultimately we are the conductor leading, balancing, arranging, and harmonizing with the orchestra of our life. It is up to us to manage the roles and parts that we play, and to allow music to help guide us back to our ultimate destination . . . our hearts!

Musical Prescriptions
for Health Index

Afterword

Chopin's Nocturnes

I BELIEVE THAT MOST OF US want to live a more heart-centered life, but sometimes it feels as if real life gets in the way. All of us have situations that come into our days that challenge us to either open our hearts and truly experience the emotions of the situation or numb ourselves. When we allow ourselves to experience the emotions, our heart expands, even though it may be painful. When we numb ourselves, the emotions eventually surface in one way or another for us to deal with. When we are in the midst of these transformational yet difficult experiences, do we underestimate the true potential of music to lead us back home to our hearts?

As I was writing this book, music has led me back home to my heart many times. I found myself re-implementing many tools I had put on the backburner and relearning many important lessons. You may have heard the saying "We teach what we need to learn most." Before this book was finished, I discovered this to be true. I still had *at least* one more major lesson to learn on my own.

With two weeks left to hand in my manuscript, I got a call from my sister that my ninety-one-year-old mom was very ill. I flew back to New Jersey to be with her and my family. When I got there, my mom was in critical care. My sister and I would sit on opposite sides of the bed, each one of us holding a separate hand, each one of us experiencing my mom's passing in a different way. Her small hands and frail fingers would grasp mine. I remember thinking these were the same fingers that guided my fingers over the piano as I sat in musical awe for the first time when I was two years old. These were the fingers that opened the door to my musical life.

Although my mom did not consider herself a musician, she *loved* music. There was a part of me that did not realize how much. I was surprised when my sister told me that two weeks prior my mom had informed her that when she died and her casket was being placed in the grave she wanted us to play Chopin's "Nocturne Opus 9 Number 2."

Two nights before my mom passed, she seemed to get a bit better and was very cognizant. As my sister and I sat with her, she could not really talk but was able to write us notes on a chalkboard. She communicated that she was worried about paying her bills. When my sister told her they were taken care of, she even knew how much of a credit the electric company owed her. The next night was not as good. My mom lost the ability to breathe on her own and passed the next morning. My sister, my nephew, and I were all in the room. I played some soft music for her and could feel her hand let go of mine. . . . Mom was gone.

Many months later, I was composing music live with Dr. Joe Dispenza at a workshop with over five hundred people. During one of the meditations, I felt my mom's energy. It's hard to explain, but it was as if she was sitting down next to me and placing her fingers on top of mine, guiding the musical notes I played, like she did the very first time. It was a very powerful experience.

It was the meditation right before lunch, and as the crowd cleared the room after it was completed I decided to stay and integrate for a moment. The audiovisual team played recorded music during the lunch break and I just allowed myself to relax with it. The next song came on and I felt moved by it and felt it move through me. I recognized it as Chopin's "Nocturne Opus 9 Number 2." I began to tear up. Mom was with me. She would always be there in this song. We would always be connected through music.

As I write the closing notes of this book, I am listening to this piece. I am feeling her heart, and I know she is feeling mine. There was a reason this book was finished after her passing. It is a powerful remembrance of the power of music to heal, transform, and touch our souls at the deepest level. To tell us everything is all right, no matter how painful. Our hearts can grow and expand through the pain if we allow them to. Like the twelve-year-old boy I was many years ago, sitting on the edge of his bed composing his first songs in bliss, music has elevated me once again and truly has created healing. Embrace music fully into your life, truly hear the secret language of the heart, and your life will be forever changed. And so it is. . . .

Acknowledgments

I AM SO THANKFUL to be able to share *The Secret Language of the Heart*. This book is dedicated to the many people who have touched my life in bringing forth this book and my music to the world.

To my love, Donese, who has taught me the beauty of bridging science and spirituality and has supported me unconditionally with her love from the day I met her. In addition, she assisted in sorting through much of the research provided in this book.

To my mother, who sparked my curiosity for music and fanned the flames of my heart to share it in the world. To my father Ben, who taught me the true meaning of the promise I made to stick with music. To my sister Lisa, who filled our home with music and paved the vibrational path for me to step into. To my brother-in-law Henry, my niece Samantha, and my nephew Jake, who all hold a very sacred space in my heart.

To Dr. Joe Dispenza, and my publisher Randy Davila, for encouraging me and mentoring me through the process of writing this book.

And to all my extended family and the many amazing teachers, sound pioneers, and authors I have had the blessing of working with who continue to teach me and touch my life.

Sample Playlists

If you're new at creating "musical prescriptions," the sample play-lists that follow are a great starting point. These are lists that have worked for me. Take a listen, have fun, and modify them to suit your tastes and needs. You may even want to interweave some of these suggestions into your own lists. Ultimately, your most power-ful experience will be in creating your own!

Gratitude

1. "Thank You for This Day" by Karen Drucker
2. "Thank You (Falettinme Be Mice Elf Agin)" by Sly and the Family Stone
3. "Angel" by Sarah McLachlan
4. "Thank You" by Dido
5. "What a Wonderful World" by Louis Armstrong
6. "Love Can Build a Bridge" by The Judds
7. "Remember" by Aleya Dao and Barry Goldstein
8. "We Are So Much More" by Elisa Brown
9. "Gratitude" by Earth, Wind & Fire
10. "Beauty in Hard Places" by Colette Baron-Reid

Joy

1. "I Want You Back" by The Jackson 5
2. "Good Vibrations" by The Beach Boys
3. "Love Train" by The O'Jays
4. "Come On Get Happy" by The Partridge Family
5. "Joy to the World" by Three Dog Night
6. "Walking on Sunshine" by Katrina & The Waves
7. "Happy" by Pharrell Williams
8. "Happy Together" by The Turtles
9. "Celebration" by Kool & The Gang
10. "Don't Worry, Be Happy" by Bobby McFerrin

Inspiration

1. "I Am Light" by India.Arie
2. "Love Can Build a Bridge" by The Judds
3. "Unwritten" by Natasha Bedingfield
4. "You Gotta Be" by Des'ree
5. "Reach" by Gloria Estefan
6. "I Believe I Can Fly" by R. Kelly
7. "Heal the World" by Michael Jackson
8. "Somewhere Over the Rainbow" by Israel Kamakawiwo'ole
9. "True Colors" by Cyndi Lauper
10. "This Little Light of Mine" by Faith Rivera

Peace

1. "Om Shree Saché" by Deva Premal
2. "Watermark" by Enya
3. "In the Om Zone" by Steven Halpern
4. "Imagine" by John Lennon
5. "Peace Train" by Cat Stevens
6. "Let Peace Prevail on Earth" James Twyman

7. "East Meets West" by Peter Sterling
8. "Om Shanti" by Rickie Byars Beckwith
9. "Ballad of Buddha Blue" by Martha Reich with Gregg Braden and Michael Kott
10. "The Breath of Peace" by Barry Goldstein

Relaxation

1. "Haven of Peace" by Constance Demby
2 "Touching Calm" by Liquid Mind
3. "Dreamscape" by Diane Arkenstone
4. "Jai Radha Madhav" by Deva Premal
5. "Genesis" by Barry Goldstein
6. "Holy Harmony" by Jonathan Goldman
7. "Illumination of the Heart" by Deuter
8. "Relaxation Suite VII" by Steven Halpern
9. "Visionary Temples" by Dean Evenson & Scott Huckabay
10. *Music to Change Your Brain: Deep Sleep* by Dr. Jeffrey Thompson

Motivation

1. "Messiah" by Handel
2. "Chariots of Fire" by Vangelis
3. "Return to Innocence" by Enigma
4. "Be the Change" MC Yogi
5. "Love Is" by Laurell Eden
6. "I Choose Love" by Shawn Gallaway
7. "I Will Survive" by Gloria Gaynor
8. "Gonna Fly Now" by Bill Conti
9. "Ignite the Heart" by Barry Goldstein
10. "Firework" by Katy Perry

For the Energy Centers

1. Base (Root): "Drum Dance" by Barry Goldstein
2. Sacral: "Swadhisthana" by Vive
3. Solar Plexus: "Conquest of Paradise" by Vangelis
4. Heart: "Shores of Avalon" by Tina Malia
5. Throat: "Om Namo Narayanaya" by Deva Premal
6. Third Eye: "Third Eye Chakra Light Vision" by Dean Evenson
7. Crown: "The Light (Crown Chakra)" by Michael Chorvat

Notes

1   MA Rollin McCraty, Mike Atkinson, William A. Tiller, Glen Rein, and Alan D Watkins, "The Effects of Emotions on Short-Term Power Spectrum Analysis of Heart Rate Variability," *American Journal of Cardiology* 76, nos. 14, 15 (November 1995): 1089–93.

2   Anita L Gadberry, "Steady Beat and State Anxiety," *Journal of Music Therapy* 48, no. 3 (September 2011): 346–56, doi: 10.1093/jmt/48.3.346.

3   HJ Trappe, "The Effects of Music on the Cardiovascular System and Cardiovascular Health," *Heart* 96, no. 23 (December 2010): 1868–71, doi: 10.1136/hrt.2010.209858; Crippa Giuseppe, Crippa Camillo, Cassi Antonino, and Luisa Fares Maria, "Effect of Music Listening During Blood Pressure Measurement," *Journal of Clinical Hypertension* 14, Supplement (May 2012): 1–10.

4   Björn Vickhoff, Helge Malmgren, Rickard Åström, Gunnar Nyberg, Seth-Reino Ekström, Mathias Engwall, Johan Snygg, Michael Nilsson, and Rebecka Jörnsten, "Music Structure Determines Heart Rate Variability of Singers," *Front Psychology* 4 (September 2013): 599, doi: 10.3389/fpsyg.2013.00334.

5   YC Lee, CY Lei, YS Shih, WC Zhang, HM Wang, CL Tseng, MC Hou, HY Chiang, and SC Huang, "HRV Response of Vegetative State Patient with Music Therapy," *Conference Proceedings: Annual International Conference of the IEEE Engineering in Medicine and Biology Society* (2011): 1701–4, doi: 10.1109/IEMBS.2011.6090488.

6   Jon Lieff, "Music Stimulates Emotions Through Specific Brain Circuits." March 2, 2014. http://jonlieffmd.com/blog/music-stimulates-emotions-through-specific-brain-circuits.

7   C Grape, M Sandgren, LO Hansson, M Ericson, and T Theorell, "Does Singing Promote Well-Being?: An Empirical Study of Professional and Amateur Singers During a Singing Lesson," *Integrative Physiological and Behavioral Science* 38, no. 1 (January–March 2003): 65–74.

8   VN Salimpoor, M Benovoy, L Larcher, A Dagher, and RJ Zatorre, "Anatomically Distinct Dopamine Release During Anticipation and Experience of Peak Emotion to Music," *Nature Neuroscience* 14, no. 2 (February 2011): 257–62, doi: 10.1038/nn.2726.

9 A Katagiri, "The Effect of Background Music and Song Texts on the Emotional Understanding of Children with Autism," *Journal of Music Therapy* 46, no. 1 (Spring 2009): 15–31.

10 Petr Janata, "The Neural Architecture of Music-Evoked Autobiographical Memories," *Cerebral Cortex* 19, no. 11 (November 2009): 2579–94, doi: 10.1093/cercor/bhp008.

11 "Definition of Neuroplasticity," MedicineNet.com, http://www.medicinenet.com/script/main/art.asp?articlekey=40362. Last updated June 14, 2012.

12 Betty A Bailey and Jane W Davidson, "Effects of Group Singing and Performance for Marginalized and Middle-Class Singers," *Psychology of Music* 33, no. 3 (July 2005): 269–303, doi: 10.1177/0305735605053734.

13 BG Kalyani, G Venkatasubramanian, R Arasappa, NP Rao, SV Kalmady, RV Behere, H Rao, MK Vasudev, and BN Gangadhar, "Neurohemodynamic Correlates of 'OM' Chanting: A Pilot Functional Magnetic Resonance Imaging Study," *International Journal of Yoga* 4, no. 1 (January 2011): 3–6, doi: 10.4103/0973-6131.78171.

14 Melinda Maxfield, PhD, "Drumming and Brain Wave Study Presentation Abstract," from Brainwave Entrainment to External Rhythmic Stimuli: Interdisciplinary Research and Clinical Perspectives, a symposium held May 13, 2006 at Stanford University's Center for Computer Research in Music and Acoustics (CCRMA).

15 Ping Ho, Jennie CI Tsao, Lian Bloch, and Lonnie K Zeltzer, "The Impact of Group Drumming on Social-Emotional Behavior in Low-Income Children," *Evidence-Based Complementary and Alternative Medicine* (2011), doi: 10.1093/ecam/neq072.

16 Spargo, Mary. "Translation of Slave Songs." *Detroit News* (1997). http://historyengine.richmond.edu/episodes/view/4844.

17 VN Salimpoor, M Benovoy, K Larcher, A Dagher, and RJ Zatorre, "Anatomically Distinct Dopamine Release During Anticipation and Experience of Peak Emotion to Music," *Nature Neuroscience* 14, no. 2 (February 2011): 257–62. doi: 10.1038/nn.2726.

18 DS Khalsa, D Amen, C Hanks, N Money, and A Newberg, "Cerebral Blood Flow Changes During Chanting Meditation," *Nuclear Medicine Communications* 30, no. 12 (December 2009): 956–61, doi: 10.1097/MNM.0b013e32832fa26c; V Khode and A Mooventhan, "Effect of Bhramari Pranayama and OM Chanting on Pulmonary Function in Healthy Individuals: A Prospective Randomized Control Trial," *International Journal of Yoga* 7, no. 2 (July 2014): 104–10, doi: 10.4103/0973-6131.133875.

19 AM Kumar, F Tims, DG Cruess, MJ Mintzer, G Ironson, D Loewenstein, R Cattan, JB Fernandez, C Eisdorfer, and M Kumar, "Music Therapy Increases Serum Melatonin Levels in Patients with Alzheimer's Disease," *Alternative Therapies in Health and Medicine* 5, no. 6 (November 1999): 49–57.

20 Naomi Ziv, Amit Granot, Sharon Hai, Ayelet Dassa, and Iris Haimov, "The Effect of Background Stimulative Music on Behavior in Alzheimer's Patients," *Journal of Music Therapy* 44, no. 4 (Winter 2007): 329–43.

21 VN Salimpoor, M Benovoy, K Larcher, A Dagher, and RJ Zatorre, "Anatomically Distinct Dopamine Release During Anticipation and Experience of Peak Emotion to Music," *Nature Neuroscience* 14, no. 2 (February 2011): 257–62, doi: 10.1038/nn.2726.

22 J Katagiri, "The Effect of Background Music and Song Texts on the Emotional Understanding of Children with Autism," *Journal of Music Therapy* 46, no. 1 (Spring 2009): 15–31; Grace Lai, Spiro P Pantazatos, Harry Schneider, and Joy Hirsch, "Neural Systems for Speech and Song in Autism," *Brain* 135 (March 2012): 961–75.

23 Amy Kalas, "Joint Attention Responses of Children with Autism Spectrum Disorder to Simple versus Complex Music," *Journal of Music Therapy* 49, no. 4 (2012): 430–452, doi: 10.1093/jmt/49.4.430.

24 S Ezzone, C Baker, R Rosselet, and E Terepka, "Music as an Adjunct to Antiemetic Therapy," *Oncology Nursing Forum* 25, no. 9 (October 1998): 1551–6.

25 N Gale, S Enright, C Reagon, I Lewis, and R van Deursen, "A Pilot Investigation of Quality of Life and Lung Function Following Choral Singing in Cancer Survivors and Their Caretakers," *ecancermedicalscience* 6 (2012): 261, doi: 10.3332/ecancer.2012.261.

26 U Nilsson, "Soothing Music Can Increase Oxytocin Levels During Bed Rest After Open-Heart Surgery: A Randomised Control Trial," *Journal of Clinical Nursing* 18, no. 15 (August 2009): 2153–61, doi: 10.1111/j.1365-2702.2008.02718.x.

27 HJ Trappe, "The Effects of Music on the Cardiovascular System and Cardiovascular Health," *Heart* 96, no. 23 (December 2010): 1868–71, doi: 10.1136/hrt.2010.209858.

28 M Miller, CC Mangano, V Beach, WJ Kop, and RA Vogel, "Divergent Effects of Joyful and Anxiety-Provoking Music on Endothelial Vasoreactivity," *Psychosomatic Medicine* 72, no. 4 (May 2010): 354–6, doi: 10.1097/PSY.0b013e3181da7968.

29 HC Sung, AM Chang, and J Abbey, "Application of Music Therapy for Managing Agitated Behavior in Older People with Dementia," *Hu Li Za Zhi* 53, no. 5 (October 2006): 58–62.

30 "Music, Art, and Alzheimer's," Alzheimer's Association, http://www.alz.org/care/alzheimers-dementia-music-art-therapy.asp#ixzz3L2kUgCCS.

31 Tanja Bekhuis, "Music Therapy May Reduce Pain and Anxiety in Children Undergoing Medical and Dental Procedures," *Journal of Evidence-Based Dental Practice* 9, no. 4 (December 2009): 213–4, doi: 10.1016/j.jebdp.2009.03.002.

32 S Coulton, S Clift, A Skingley, and J Rodriguez, "Effectiveness and Cost-Effectiveness of Community Singing on Mental Health-Related Quality of Life of Older People: Randomised Controlled Trial," *British Journal of Psychiatry* 207, no. 3 (September 2015): 250–5, doi: 10.1192/bjp.bp.113.129908.

33 CF Wang, YL Sun, and HX Zang, "Music Therapy Improves Sleep Quality in Acute and Chronic Sleep Disorders: A Meta-analysis of 10 Randomized Studies," *International Journal of Nursing Studies* 51, no. 1 (January 2014): 51–62, doi: 10.1016/j.ijnurstu.2013.03.008.

34 S Kulkarni, PC Johnson, S Kettles, and RS Kasthuri, "Music During Interventional Radiological Procedures, Effect on Sedation, Pain and Anxiety: A Randomised Controlled Trial." *British Journal of Radiology* 85, no. 1016 (August 2012): 1059–63, doi: 10.1259/bjr/71897605.

35 EA Garza-Villarreal, AD Wilson, L Vase, E Brattico, FA Barrios, TS Jensen, J Romero-Romo, and P Vuust. "Music Reduces Pain and Increases Functional Mobility in Fibromyalgia," *Frontiers in Psychology* 5, no. 90 (February 11, 2014), doi: 10.3389/fpsyg.2014.00090.

36 G Polt, M Fink, H Schieder, S Tanzmeister, "Influence of Music on the Quality of Life of Palliative Cancer Patients" [Article in German], *Wiener Medizinische Wochenschrift* 164, nos. 9–10 (May 2014): 179–83, doi: 10.1007/s10354-014-0272-2; RE Hillard, "The Effects of Music Therapy on the Quality and Length of Life of People Diagnosed with Terminal Cancer," *Journal of Music Therapy* 40, no. 2 (Summer 2003): 113–37; MT Halstead and ST Roscoe, "Restoring the Spirit at the End of Life: Music as an Intervention for Oncology Nurses," *Clinical Journal of Oncology Nursing* 6, no. 6 (November–December 2002): 332–6.

37 C Pacchetti, F Mancini, R Aglieri, C Fundarò, E Martignoni, and G Nappi, "Active Music Therapy in Parkinson's Disease: An Integrative Method for Motor and Emotional Rehabilitation," *Psychosomatic Medicine* 62, no. 3 (May–June 2000): 386–93.

38 Kathrynne Holden, "Drum Therapy Program Helping Parkinson's Patients," National Parkinson Foundation, last updated July 24, 2011, http://forum.parkinson.org/index.php?/topic/11352-drum-therapy-program-helping-parkinsons-patients/.

39 MJ Hove, K Suzuki, H Uchitomi, S Orimo, and Y Miyake, "Interactive Rhythmic Auditory Stimulation Reinstates Natural 1/f Timing in Gait of Parkinson's Patients," European Parkinson's Association, March 2, 2012, http://www.epda.eu.com/en/research-papers/2012/plosone/03-02-plosone/.

40 BS Kisilevsky, SMJ Hains, AY Jacquet, C Granier-Deferre, and JP Lecanuet, "Maturation of Fetal Responses to Music," *Developmental Science* 7 no. 5 (2004): 550–59; DK James, CJ Spencer, and BW Stepsis, "Fetal Learning: A Prospective Randomized Controlled Study," *Ultrasound Obstetrics Gynecology* 20 no. 5 (November 2002): 431–8; RP Cooper and RN Aslin, "The Language Environment of the Young Infant: Implications for Early Perceptual Development," *Canadian Journal of Experimental Psychology* 43 no. 2 (June 1989): 247–65; S Simavli, I Gumus, I Kaygusuz, M Yildirim, B Usluogullari, and H Kafali, "Effect of Music on Labor

Pain Relief, Anxiety Level and Postpartum Analgesic Requirement: A Randomized Controlled Clinical Trial," *Gynecologic and Obstetric Investigation* 78 no. 4 (2014): 244–50, doi: 10.1159/000365085.

41 Kisilevsky, et al., "Maturation of Fetal Responses to Music."

42 MJ Silverman, "The Influence of Music on the Symptoms of Psychosis: A Meta-analysis," *Journal of Music Therapy* 40 no. 1 (Spring 2003): 27–40.

43 S Khalfa, SD Bella, M Roy, I Peretz, and SJ Lupien, "Effects of Relaxing Music on Salivary Cortisol Level After Psychological Stress," *Annals of the New York Academy of Sciences* 999 (November 2003): 374–6.

44 Monika Jungblut, Walter Huber, Christiane Mais, and Ralph Schnitker, "Paving the Way for Speech: Voice-Training-Induced Plasticity in Chronic Aphasia and Apraxia of Speech—Three Single Cases," *Neural Plasticity* (2014), doi: 10.1155/2014/841982.

45 M Villeneuve, V Penhune, and A Lamontagne, "A Piano Training Program to Improve Manual Dexterity and Upper Extremity Function in Chronic Stroke Survivors," *Frontiers in Human Neuroscience* 8 (August 22, 2014): 662, doi: 10.3389/fnhum.2014.00662.

46 "How Can Music Therapy Help Stroke Survivors?" The Stroke Foundation, last accessed October 28, 2015, http://www.thestrokefoundation.com/index.php/music-and-stroke/22-how-can-music-therapy-help-stroke-survivors.

References

Baird, A, and S Samson, "Music evoked autobiographical memory after severe acquired brain injury": Preliminary findings from a case series, Neuropsychological Rehabilitation, Epub 2013 Nov 21.

Baker, Mitzi. "Music Moves Brain to Pay Attention, Stanford Study Finds." Stanford Medicine News Center. August 1, 2007. http://med.stanford.edu/news_releases/2007/july/music.html.

Baker, SL. "Music Benefits the Brain, Research Reveals." *Natural News*. July 30, 2010. http://www.naturalnews.com/029324_music_brain.html.

Blood, Anne J, and Robert J Zatorre. "Intensely Pleasurable Responses to Music Correlate with Activity in Brain Regions Implicated in Reward and Emotion." *Proceedings of the National Academy of Sciences* 98, no. 20 (September 25, 2001): 11818–23. doi: 10.1073/pnas.191355898.

Calaprice, Alice. *The Ultimate Quotable Einstein*. Princeton, NJ: Princeton University Press, 2013.

Campbell, Don. *The Mozart Effect for Children: Awakening Your Child's Mind, Health, and Creativity with Music*. New York: HarperCollins, 2000.

Chanda, ML, and DJ Levitin. "The Neurochemistry of Music." *Trends in Cognitive Sciences* 17, no. 4 (April 2013): 179–93. doi: 10.1016/j.tics.2013.02.007. Review.

Chang, En-Ting, Hui-Ling Lai, Pin-Wen Chen, Yuan-Mei Hsieh, and Li-Hua Lee. "The Effects of Music on the Sleep Quality of Adults with Chronic Insomnia Using Evidence from Polysomnographic and Self-Reported Analysis: A Randomized Control Trial." *International Journal of Nursing Studies* 49, no. 8 (August 2012): 921–30. doi: 10.1016/j.ijnurstu.2012.02.019.

Chevalier, Gaétan, Stephen T Sinatra, James L Oschman, Karol Sokal, and Pawel Sokal. "Earthing: Health Implications of Reconnecting the Human Body to the Earth's Surface Electrons." *Journal of Environmental and Public Health* (January 12, 2012). doi: 10.1155/2012/291541.

"Circadian Rhythms Fact Sheet." National Institute of General Medical Sciences. March 6, 2014. http://www.nigms.nih.gov/Education/Pages/Factsheet_Circadian Rhythms.aspx.

Fedyniak, Lev G. "A Cat's Purr." Living Water Natural Healing & Health Solutions. http://www.livingwaterhealthsolutions.com/Articles/catsPurr.php.

Foster, Brian. "Einstein and His Love of Music." *Physics World* 18, no. 1 (January 2005): 34. http://www.anu.edu.au/physics/Savage/TEE/site/tee/learning/media/physics_ world_18_1b.pdf.

Gadberry, AL. "Steady Beat and State Anxiety." *Journal of Music Therapy* 48, no. 3 (Fall 2011): 346–56.

Gazzaley Lab, "Rhythm and the Brain Project – A Gazzaley – Hart Collaboration," http://gazzaleylab.ucsf.edu/neuroscience-projects/rhythm-brain-project/.

Gibson, Crystal, Bradley S. Folley, and Sohee Park. "Enhanced Divergent Thinking and Creativity in Musicians: A Behavioral and Near-Infrared Spectroscopy Study." *Brain and Cognition* 69 (2009): 162–69.

HeartMath. "How Stress Affects the Body," http://www.heartmath.com/infographics/ how-stress-effects-the-body/.

Horn, Stacy. "Singing Changes Your Brain." *Time* (August 16, 2013). http://ideas.time. com/2013/08/16/singing-changes-your-brain/.

Janata, Petr. "The Neural Architecture of Music-Evoked Autobiographical Memories." *Cerebral Cortex* (2009). doi: 10.1093/cercor/bhp008.

Katagiri, J. "The Effect of Background Music and Song Texts on the Emotional Understanding of Children with Autism" *Journal of Music Therapy* 46, no. 1 (Spring 2009): 15–31.

Lengacher, CA, MP Bennett, and L Gonzalez. "Immune Responses to Guided Imagery During Breast Cancer Treatment." *Biological Research for Nursing* 9, no. 3 (2008): 205–14. doi:10.1177/1099800407309374.

Lesiuk, Teresa. "The Effect of Preferred Music on Mood and Performance in a High-Cognitive Demand Occupation." *Journal of Music Therapy* 47, no. 2 (Summer 2010): 137–54.

Limb, CJ, and AR Braun. "Neural Substrates of Spontaneous Musical Performance: An FMRI Study of Jazz Improvisation" *PLoS One* 3, no. 2 (February 27, 2008): 1679. doi: 10.1371/journal.pone.0001679.

Lieff, Jon. "Music Stimulates Emotions Through Specific Brain Circuits." March 2, 2014. http://jonlieffmd.com/blog/music-stimulates-emotions-through-specific-brain-circuits.

Maack, C, and P Nolan. "The Effects of Guided Imagery and Music Therapy on Reported Change in Normal Adults." *Journal of Music Therapy* 36, no. 1 (1999): 39–55.

Mavridis, IN. "Music and the Nucleus Accumbens." *Surgical and Radiologic Anatomy* 37, no. 2 (March 2015): 121–5. doi: 10.1007/s00276-014-1360-0.

Moisse, Katie, Bob Woodruff, James Hill, and Lana Zak. "Gabby Giffords: Finding Words Through Song." November 11, 2011. http://abcnews.go.com/Health/ w_MindBodyNews/gabby-giffords-finding-voice-music-therapy/story?id =14903987.

"Neuroscience of Music—How Music Enhances Learning Through Neuroplasticity." NeuroscienceNews.com.July20,2010.http://neurosciencenews.com/neuroscience -music-enchances-learning-neuroplasticity/.

O'Brien, Jane. "Power of Art: Can Music Help Treat Children with Attention Disorders?" BBC News, Washington. http://www.bbc.com/news/magazine-21661689. March 5, 2013.

"Research FAQs." Institute of HeartMath, http://www.heartmath.org/faqs/research/ research-faqs.html.

Roberts, Melina, and Katrina McFerran. "A Mixed Methods Analysis of Songs Written by Bereaved Preadolescents in Individual Music Therapy." *Journal of Music Therapy* 50, no.1 (Spring 2013): 25–52.

Schlesinger, Ilana, Orna Benyakov, Ilana Erikh, and Maria Nassar. "Relaxation Guided Imagery Reduces Motor Fluctuations in Parkinson's Disease." *Journal of Parkinson's Disease* 4, no. 3 (2014): 431–6. doi: 10.3233/JPD-130338.

Shih, YN, RH Huang, and HY Chiang. "Background Music: Effects on Attention Performance." *Work* 42, no. 4 (2012): 573–8. doi: 10.3233/WOR-2012-1410.

Shulman, Matthew. "Music as Medicine for the Brain." U.S. News & World Report. July 17, 2008. http://health.usnews.com/health-news/family-health/brain-and-behavior/articles/2008/07/17/music-as-medicine-for-the-brain.

Spargo, Mary. "Translation of Slave Songs." Detroit News (1997). http://historyengine. richmond.edu/episodes/view/4844.

Sung, Huei-Chuan, Anne M Chang, and Jennifer Abbey. "Application of Music Therapy for Managing Agitated Behavior in Older People with Dementia." *Hu Li Za Zhi* 53, no. 5 (October 2006): 58–62. [Article in Chinese. Abstract available in English at http://www.ncbi.nlm.nih.gov/pubmed/17004208.]

"The Effects of Stress on Your Body." WebMD. http://www.webmd.com/mental-health/ effects-of-stress-on-your-body.

Whipple, Jennifer. "Music in Intervention for Children and Adolescents with Autism: A Meta-Analysis." *Journal of Music Therapy* 41, no. 2 (Summer 2004): 90–106.

Ziv, Naomi, Amit Granot, Saron Hai, Ayelet Dassa, and Iris Haimov. "The Effect of Background Simulative Music on Behavior in Alzheimer's Patients." *Journal of Music Therapy* 44, no. 4 (Winter 2007): 329–43.

Music Resources by the Author

Ambiology 1: The Heart

Ambiology 2: The Breath

Ambiology 3: The Journey

Ambiology 4: Home

Ambiology 5: Eden

Ambiology 6: Genesis

Ambiology for Pets

The Heart Codes

Shine

The Sound of Joy

The Moment

Butterfly Transformation

Peaceful Day

Wisdom Of The Heart (Monroe Institute)

Your Heart's Song (Monroe Institute)

Cosmic Consciousness (Monroe Institute)

Element 5: The Lost Key

There's an Angel Watching You

Ignite The Heart

A Musical Voyage to Cosmic Consciousness

The Secret Language of the Heart Volumes 1 and 2

About the Author

Barry Goldstein has been a composer, producer, and researcher on the vibrational effects of music for more than twenty-five years. He brings his knowledge of frequency, resonance, entrainment, and harmonics into his healing with music series Ambiology, which is being used in hospitals, hospices, medical offices, and in individuals' homes worldwide. He is a Billboard Top Ten recording artist, and his work spans many styles and genres, from coproducing the Grammy Award–winning track "69 Freedom Special" with Les Paul to providing original ambient music for Shirley MacLaine, Neale Donald Walsch, Gregg Braden, Dr. Joe Dispenza, and Dr. Daniel Amen. Research on the benefits of Barry's music is currently being conducted, and Barry is a sought-after speaker for medical and motivational conferences.